Bill Bright had one goal in life: to share the good news of Jesus Christ with as many people as possible and by every means possible.

From the Foreword by
BILLY GRAHAM

# BILL BRIGHT'S
# "THE JOY OF KNOWING GOD"
# SERIES

# the JOY of TRUSTING GOD

## DR. BILL BRIGHT

*Victor*®

*The Bible Teacher's Teacher*

COOK COMMUNICATIONS MINISTRIES
Colorado Springs, Colorado • Paris, Ontario
KINGSWAY COMMUNICATIONS LTD
Eastbourne, England

Victor® is an imprint of
Cook Communications Ministries,
Colorado Springs, CO 80918
Cook Communications, Paris, Ontario
Kingsway Communications, Eastbourne, England

THE JOY OF TRUSTING GOD
© 2005 by Bill Bright

First Printing, 2005
Printed in United States of America
1 2 3 4 5 6 7 8 9 10 Printing/Year 09 08 07 06 05

Cover Design: Brand Navigation, LLC

Unless otherwise identified, Scripture quotations
are taken from the Holy Bible. New Living Translation
copyright © 1996 by Tyndale Charitable Trust.
Used by permission of Tyndale House Publishers.
Other versions used include the HOLY BIBLE, NEW
INTERNATIONAL VERSION®. (NIV). Copyright © 1973, 1978, 1984
International Bible Society. Used by permission of Zondervan. All rights
reserved; and the New King James Version®. (NKJV). Copyright © 1982
by Thomas Nelson, Inc. Used by permission. All rights reserved. Italics
used in Scripture are added for author's emphasis.

Library of Congress Cataloging-in-Publication Data

Bright, Bill.
 The joy of trusting God : character you can count on / Bill Bright.
     p. cm. -- (The joy of knowing God series ; bk. 1)
 ISBN 0-7814-4246-X (pbk.)
 1. Trust in God--Christianity. I. Title. II. Series.

BV4637.B75 2005
231.7--dc22

                                                       2004027058

# Dedication

## GLOBAL FOUNDING PARTNERS

*The Bright Media Foundation continues the multifaceted ministries of Bill and Vonette Bright for generations yet unborn. God has touched and inspired the Brights through the ministries of writers through the centuries. Likewise, they wish to pass along God's message in Jesus Christ as they have experienced it, seeking to inspire, train, and transform lives, thereby helping to fulfill the Great Commission each year until our Lord returns.*

*Many generous friends have prayed and sacrificed to support the Bright Media Foundation's culturally relevant, creative works, in print and electronic forms. The following persons specifically have helped to establish the foundation. These special friends will always be known as* Global Founding Partners *of the Bright Media Foundation.*

*Bill and Christie Heavener and family*

*Stuart and Debra Sue Irby and family*

*Edward E. Haddock Jr., Edye Murphy-Haddock, and the Haddock family*

# Acknowledgments

It was my privilege to share fifty-four years, six months, and twenty days of married life with a man who loved Jesus passionately and served Him faithfully. Six months before his home going, Bill initiated what has become "The Joy of Knowing God" series. It was his desire to pass along to future generations the insights God had given him that they, too, could discover God's magnificence and live out the wonderful plan He has for their lives.

"The Joy of Knowing God" series is a collection of Bill Bright's top ten life-changing messages. Millions of people around the world have already benefited greatly from these spiritual truths and are now living the exciting Christian adventure that God desires for each of us.

On behalf of Bill, I want to thank the following team that helped research, compile, edit, and wordsmith the manuscripts and audio scripts in this series: Jim Bramlett, Rebecca Cotton, Eric Metaxas, Sheryl Moon, Cecil Price, Michael Richardson, Eric Stanford, and Rob Suggs.

I also want to thank Bill's longtime friends and Campus Crusade associates Bailey Marks and Ted Martin, who carefully reviewed the scripts and manuscripts for accuracy.

Bill was deeply grateful to Bob Angelotti and Don Stillman of Allegiant Marketing Group for their encouragement to produce this series and their ingenuity in facilitating distribution to so many.

A special thanks to Cook Communications and its team of dedicated professionals who partnered with Bright Media Foundation in this venture, as well as to Steve Laube, who brought us together.

Last but not least, I want to express my appreciation to Helmut Teichert, who worked faithfully and diligently in overseeing this team that Bill's vision would be realized, and to John Nill, CEO of Bright Media, who has helped me navigate the many challenges along this journey.

As a result of the hard work of so many, and especially our wonderful Lord's promise of His grace, I trust that multitudes worldwide will experience a greater joy by knowing God and His ways more fully.

With a grateful heart,
MRS. BILL BRIGHT (VONETTE)

# Contents

# Foreword

One of the greatest experiences of my life has been the privilege of knowing Bill and Vonette Bright. Not only have they been friends to Ruth and me, but over the years few people have encouraged and supported us more. I rejoice that Bill is now in the presence of the Lord he served so faithfully—but I am going to miss him.

I think Bill Bright was one of the most focused people I ever knew. He had one goal in life: to share the good news of Jesus Christ with as many people as possible and by every means possible. His vision, his single-mindedness, and his dedication were a constant example to me and to countless others whose lives he touched across the world.

I first met Bill in 1949 at the home of Henrietta Mears, a gifted Bible teacher with a deep burden to win young people to Christ. One evening she invited me to one of her Bible classes, and there I met Bill and Vonette. He was helping Henrietta and also working with students at UCLA. I was thrilled as God used Bill and Vonette to build Campus Crusade for Christ into one of the great Christian organizations in the world.

Bill always sought to build his life and his ministry on the Scriptures and on prayer. He extended the hand of fellowship to all believers, whatever their background. Many times Bill would call me on the phone or come to see me, just to encourage me in the work of the Lord. He always left me with a Scripture verse, and I knew he was always praying for me.

Bill would often come to our crusades, and he participated

also in the various evangelism conferences we sponsored. In his last illness, he showed great courage and faith and continued to minister despite his health challenges. In his last years, Bill truly experienced the reality of God's promise to the apostle Paul: "My grace is sufficient for you, for my power is made perfect in weakness" (2 Corinthians 12:9 NIV).

Now Bill's life on this earth is over. He has fought the good fight, he has finished the race, he has kept the faith. But for us the race is not over. The Great Commission has never been rescinded, and the spiritual needs of the world have never been greater. May the memory of Bill's life challenge each of us to a deeper dedication to Christ and a great zeal to spread His Word to the ends of the earth, as long as God gives us life.

— BILLY GRAHAM

# 1

# Can We Really Know God?

That is probably the most important question anyone could ever ask. And the more we think about it, the more daunting the question seems. Is it possible for a human being—a mere speck on a planet speeding through infinite space—to know the great God who created our galaxy and the 100 billion other galaxies?

It really is quite a question. But let us say it *is* possible to know Him. Can we know Him well enough to be able to trust Him with the most sensitive areas in our lives? Then an even more difficult question follows: *Do* we know Him that well—well enough to love and obey Him in whatever He asks of us?

Let me say up front, my friend, that it is my most passionate desire to help you know God, to love Him, and to serve Him. I can promise that as you do these things, you will undoubtedly experience the greatest adventure life has to offer.

## THE MOST IMPORTANT TRUTH

I f you are like me, the prospect of understanding and knowing our great God seems daunting. You might even wonder why you should attempt such a seemingly impossible task. Why should *any* of us try to understand who God is?

*Knowing God's attributes is the key to everything else in life.*

Many years ago, Dr. James Montgomery Boice interviewed me on his "Bible Hour" radio program. One of the first questions Dr. Boice asked me was, "What is the most important truth to teach any follower of Christ?"

What an incredible question! No one had ever asked me that before, so I was not prepared to answer it. For a brief moment, I was speechless—never a good thing on radio. But then the Holy Spirit gave me the answer: "the attributes of God."

I have had years to think about Dr. Boice's question and my answer. Today, I am more convinced than ever that there is indeed nothing more important to teach another believer than who God is, what He is like, and why or how He does what He does. These attributes of God can be referred to as His character, His nature, His qualities, or His personality. Knowing them is the key to everything else in life. Most importantly, knowing them is the key to knowing God himself.

### MARX AND LUTHER: TWO VIEWS OF GOD

W hat is your view of God? It's a simple fact that whether our view of God is positive or negative, that perception will absolutely affect all we do and who we are. How we view God affects everything—our attitude, choices, and behavior.

Two historical figures illustrate this point and show the remarkably different outcomes that result from divergent views of God.

## KARL MARX

Karl Marx, the father of communism, was born in Trier, Germany, in 1818. Marx was educated in German universities, and as a young man, he became the editor of a Cologne newspaper. Marx firmly denied the existence of God, believing that the individual, not God, is the highest form of being. Instead of affirming God's sovereignty and power, Marx believed that people make themselves what they are by their own efforts. According to him, *society* was the supreme agent for achieving success and fulfillment.

In *Economic and Philosophic Manuscripts of 1844,* Marx put it this way:

> All that is called history is nothing else than the process of creating man through human labour, the becoming of nature for man. Man has thus evident and irrefutable proof of his own creation by himself…. For man, man is the supreme being.

Since Marx believed that man was a god, it followed that society, composed of the common man, should rule and overthrow the reigning government by force. He and Friedrich Engels collaborated on defining the philosophical ideals that eventually formed the basis for communism.[1]

In the twentieth century, Vladimir Lenin revived Marx's ideas and brought about the overthrow of czarist rule in Russia. As we know, Joseph Stalin followed Lenin as the leader of the communist Soviet Union. Under the monstrous reigns of these men and the communist rulers who followed them, tens of millions of Russians were slaughtered by the state. But because these communist leaders believed there was no God, the individual human being had no inherent value. The state was of supreme importance. So killing and torturing in the name of the supposed greater good only followed logically. Today, of course, Marx's ideas still form the basis for totalitarian governments in many countries, including North Korea, Cuba, and China.

## MARTIN LUTHER

Now contrast the life of Karl Marx with that of Martin Luther, who was also revolutionary. Luther, too, was born in Germany—in the town of Eisleben in 1483. Luther was educated in German universities just as Marx was many years later.

Like Marx, the young Luther struggled with the concepts of authority, morality, and ethics. He desired to serve God and became a monk, but over time he grew increasingly terrified of God's wrath. Then he was drawn to a passage in the New Testament book of Romans: "It is through faith that a righteous person has life" (1:17). By faith! This simple concept entirely changed Luther's view of God. About that experience, he wrote the following:

> *As you love God and serve Him, you will undoubtedly experience the greatest adventure life has to offer.*

> At last, meditating day and night and by the mercy of God, I ... began to understand that the righteousness of God is that through which the righteous live by a gift of God, namely by faith.... Here I felt as if I were entirely born

again and had entered paradise itself through gates that had been flung open. [2]

Luther realized that the gift of salvation—God's free gift of forgiveness—was available to every single person on earth. He realized that God infinitely loves each person. God sent His Son to save every man, woman, and child who wants to be saved, which profoundly illustrated the value God gives to each individual. We are created in His image, and God himself would do anything for us, His children. What a perfect contrast to the beliefs of communism!

*We are created in His image, and God himself would do anything for us.*

Luther's subsequent teaching on salvation by faith—instead of trying to earn salvation through good works—was the beginning of the great Protestant Reformation that reshaped Europe during the next two centuries. Today, the principle of forgiveness by faith is espoused by hundreds of millions of people worldwide. In America, we owe much of our historical and religious roots to what Luther began in Germany.

## How Do *You* View God?

The examples of Luther and Marx show the outcome of differing beliefs. A false view of God leads to sin and corruption—and ultimately to unspeakable cruelty and great tragedy. On the other hand, a proper understanding of God leads to a life of blessing for oneself and many generations to follow.

Now you may be thinking, *I am no Karl Marx or Martin*

*Luther. I am not a world leader or a person with great influence.* Few people are. Yet how we view God will determine the

———————❖———————

*Nothing in life could be more important than establishing a personal relationship with God and understanding Him accurately.*

way we live and relate to others. Indeed, God cares about you and everyone around you as much as He has ever cared about anyone who ever lived.

So if you believe God considers you infinitely valuable, you will live accordingly. And you will treat others accordingly. But if you believe there is no God—or that God is some distant deity who can't be bothered with insignificant human beings—you will live accordingly, treating yourself and others with disrespect or even contempt. Someone who knows that God loves everyone infinitely will often go to great lengths to help the weakest and poorest. But the person who thinks there is no God has no reason not to put himself first and act selfishly, often horribly so.

All of our actions—like those of Karl Marx and Martin Luther—are driven by our views of God and how He interacts with us. Therefore, nothing in life could be more important than establishing a personal relationship with God and understanding Him accurately.

---

1. "Karl Marx," *The New Encyclopedia Britannica*, vol. 23 (Chicago: Encyclopedia Britannica, Inc., 1978).
2. James M. Kittleson, "The Breakthrough," *Christian History*, No. 34, p. 15.

# 2

## Knowing God Can Change Your Life

What misconceptions do you have about God that prevent you from getting to know Him better? Are you so unsure about what God is really like that you cannot trust Him completely?

Let me give you an example of someone whose view of God changed radically—and whose life changed radically as a result. I'm talking about John Newton, and his amazing story demonstrates what an accurate understanding of God can do for each of us.

### AMAZING GRACE

John Newton was born in 1725 in England. His mother was a devoted Christian, and intending for her son to enter the ministry, she worked hard to instill a deep faith in him. But Newton's mother died before his seventh birthday. As a young man, John decided to follow in the footsteps of his father, an English sea captain. He joined the British Royal Navy but was eventually discharged because of unruly behavior. To escape further problems, he moved to the western coast of Africa and worked for a slave trader. He eventually became captain of a slave ship, and like most slave ship captains, he treated his slaves despicably. What a loathsome man he had become—and what a terribly far cry from his mother's hopes and prayers for him!

On one voyage, a fierce storm severely battered Newton's ship. Sure that he would die, Newton surrendered himself to God. Miraculously, he survived, and he determined to set his life on a new course. At first, he remained a slave ship captain, but he tried to treat the slaves more humanely. Then he saw that slavery itself was abhorrent, so he gave up slave trading entirely. What's more, he went on to passionately crusade against slavery. His life changed so profoundly that he studied to become a minister, just as his mother had prayed. Newton came to be known as the "old converted sea captain." And this was all because he had personally met and come to know God.

> *When you discover God's love and plan for your life, you will never be the same.*

Probably the most famous thing Newton did was to write the hymn "Amazing Grace." In it, he described his own transformation:

Amazing grace, how sweet the sound,
That saved a wretch like me.
I once was lost, but now am found,
Was blind, but now I see.

Who else but Almighty God could change a callous slave

ship captain into a compassionate minister and antislavery crusader?

## Knowing God Intimately

The greatest truth known to mankind is this: God is a person, and we can know Him intimately.

We all live on a grand estate called Earth. As we look around at the beauty and intricacies of our residence, we marvel at the creativity and genius of the design. When we gaze up into the heavens, we are overcome with awe at the vastness of what our Creator has brought into being. Beholding our God's handiwork provides evidence of His existence and nature, but our God also wants us to know Him personally. He does not just want us to *know things* about Him; He desires intimate fellowship with us. Knowledge about someone is essential, but it is not enough. Developing a relationship with God requires desire, communication, and commitment.

### Relationship with God

How is developing a relationship with God possible? After all, God is a Spirit, outside of space and time—while we are in physical bodies, within space and time. Well, God has provided several ways. One way is through the Bible, God's Word to us. The Scriptures are God's own words to us about what He is like and what is important to Him. God has revealed himself to us through

> *Developing a relationship with God requires desire, communication, and commitment.*

His Son, Jesus, who stepped out of eternity and into time 2,000 years ago to live on this planet. For a number of years, it was possible for human beings to observe the incarnate God through their five senses as they walked with Jesus and talked with Him.

Ultimately, Jesus sacrificially died on the cross for our sins, so those sins would no longer be a barrier between our holy God and us. But when He left, He sent the Holy Spirit to live inside each one of us who receives Him as our Savior. God did all this so we could go beyond just knowing *about* Him and actually enter into an eternal friendship and family relationship with Him.

*As we grow spiritually, God makes it possible for us to become more and more intimate with Him.*

To be sure, developing intimacy with God is a growth process. When our son, Zachary, was only a few days old, my wife, Vonette, asked me to watch him. I was very tired and afraid I would go to sleep, so I took the baby in my arms to make certain that he would not roll off the bed while I slept. Later, when Vonette came back, we laughed at my naïveté. Here was Zachary, a newborn, who had neither the strength nor the ability to move one inch from where he had been placed. He could not possibly have fallen off the bed.

As Zachary grew older, he was able to roll over and then sit up. In time, he could crawl. Then he made attempts to stand, and he would fall and pick himself up. When he reached the point where he could take a step or two, we were elated at his progress. And when he could totter across the room from Vonette's protective arms to mine, we were ecstatic. Soon he began to walk more steadily, and then he learned to run. As he grew physically, his mental capabilities were also developing, so we could communicate better.

Similarly, as we grow spiritually, God makes it possible for us to become more and more intimate with Him. In fact, because God is a personal Spirit, we are to seek close fellowship with Him.

## DO YOU KNOW GOD?

Have you experienced God personally? Is He intimately involved in your life?

I have walked and talked with our loving heavenly Father for more than fifty years, and it has been the greatest adventure I could imagine. The more I get to know Him, the more peace, joy, love, and excitement I experience. He has proved to be my best friend, someone I can trust in every situation.

> *The more I get to know God, the more peace, joy, love, and excitement I experience.*

My desire is not just to share information about God with you—although that is important—but I want to communicate my heart to you. When you discover His love and plan for your life, you will never be the same.

————————❖————————

"YOU WILL SEEK ME AND FIND ME WHEN
YOU SEEK ME WITH ALL YOUR HEART."

JEREMIAH 29:13 NIV

————————————————

# 3

# How to Know God

It is my deepest hope that you will be encouraged to see who God really is and come to know Him well enough to love, trust, and obey Him as never before. Knowing God is the most important thing a human being can ever do.

## THREE PREREQUISITES TO KNOWING GOD

Before any of us can truly know God, we must fulfill three prerequisites.

### YOU MUST BE BORN SPIRITUALLY

The Bible tells us that we must be reborn spiritually. Although God is a person, He does not have a body. He is not a material being. So we must relate to Him Spirit to spirit. In John 4:24, Jesus told His disciples, "God is Spirit, so those who worship him must worship in spirit and in truth."

In the third chapter of John, Jesus explained spiritual birth to Nicodemus, a religious leader who had sought Him out.

————————❖————————

*We will draw close to God only*
*when we permit the Holy Spirit*
*to control us and give us*
*supernatural insight.*

————————————————

Jesus replied, "I assure
you, unless you are born
again, you can never see
the Kingdom of God."

"What do you mean?"
exclaimed Nicodemus.
"How can an old man go back into his mother's womb and
be born again?"

Jesus replied, "The truth is, no one can enter the
Kingdom of God without being born of water and the
Spirit. Humans can reproduce only human life, but the
Holy Spirit gives new life from heaven."

JOHN 3:3–6

If you have never been born again spiritually—by asking
Jesus Christ to forgive all your sins and inviting Him to come
into your life as your Savior and Lord—then I encourage you
to do so today.

### YOU MUST BE FILLED WITH THE HOLY SPIRIT

We will draw close to God only when we permit the Holy Spirit
to control us and give us supernatural insight. Jesus promised
His disciples that He would send the Holy Spirit, who would
be their counselor and reveal truth to them. In 1 Corinthians
2:10, the apostle Paul writes, "We know these things because
God has revealed them to us by his Spirit, and his Spirit
searches out everything and shows us even God's deep
secrets." Without the Holy Spirit's help, it is impossible for us
to comprehend spiritual truth.

## *You Must Seek Him with Your Whole Heart*

God's Word promises, "You will seek me and find me when you seek me with all your heart" (Jeremiah 29:13 NIV). And in Hebrews 11:6, we are promised that God "rewards those who sincerely seek him."

One way we demonstrate our sincerity in seeking God is by our commitment to reading His Word. It is not possible to really know God without listening to Him. That is what we do when we consistently spend time in the Scriptures. It is cleansing, informative, and challenging. And it is vital. The psalmist said, "I will study your commandments and reflect on your ways. I will delight in your principles and not forget your word" (119:15–16).

Another way we demonstrate our sincerity in seeking God is by obedience—simply doing what He tells us to do. Jesus promised, "Those who obey my commandments are the ones who love me. And because they love me, my Father will love them, and I will love them. And I will reveal myself to each one of them" (John 14:21). Sin, rebellion, and disobedience blind us to the light of God's magnificence. If you want to get closer to God and know Him intimately, then you must be willing to obey Him in all things.

## SERVE GOD WHOLEHEARTEDLY

Vonette and I made a commitment early in our marriage to be wholehearted in our devotion to Jesus. It is a story I have told hundreds of times. One Sunday, I had left her waiting at church after the service for three hours while I counseled someone. Poor Vonette had no idea where I was. Needless to say, when I did finally arrive, we had an intense discussion. Soon the discussion began to focus on the expectations that we had for each other in our marriage. I suggested to Vonette that we each take a sheet of paper and go to a different room and write down our expectations before God. So we did.

---❖---

*Without the Holy Spirit's help, it is impossible for us to comprehend spiritual truth.*

Vonette, who is so practical, wrote down some fundamental goals for our marriage, such as having a roof over our heads, raising children, and living a life that pleases God.

I, on the other hand, was wrestling with what I really wanted out of life. I decided to renounce every single thing to the control of the Lord Jesus Christ. I placed my life, Vonette, our family, home, car, business, and future plans entirely under the ownership of Jesus. I declared in writing that I was assuming the position of a bond slave to the Lord Jesus Christ, like the apostle Paul, and that whatever my Master would tell me to do, I would do it. I would be wholehearted in my devotion.

When we got together again and compared our papers, they were quite different. We each recognized the validity of the other's goals before God. Then we agreed that in an act of faith, we would sign those papers as an expression of our devotion to God.

Establishing that contract with God was a major spiritual milestone for Vonette and me. We were saying, "God, we want to follow You wholeheartedly, no matter what the cost. We want to obey You in everything." As a result, we have experienced God's most incredible blessings during these many years—the main one being that we have grown in our intimacy with Him.

How important is it to you to know God intimately? Are you willing to be wholehearted in serving Him? Your way of expressing your commitment may not be through a contract as Vonette and I did. But you must take the lordship of Jesus Christ seriously. That means obeying Him in every area of your life. When you make that commitment to serve God and know Him intimately, you will receive power and freedom. If you want to know God intimately, you must be willing to seek Him wholeheartedly.

## FOUR INCOMPREHENSIBLE QUALITIES OF GOD

You and I have lived our entire lives within the boundaries of time and space. As a result, we do not even have reference points to help us understand certain aspects of God's nature. Consequently, some of God's qualities can be particularly incredible.

The first one is that God is infinite, the second that He is self-existent, the third that He is eternal, and the fourth that He is self-sufficient. These four traits of God are difficult for us to understand, but they are important to try to grasp because they relate to every other aspect of God. Let me briefly describe each of these characteristics.

*God cannot be measured or compared to any finite standard.*

### GOD IS INFINITE

This means that He has no limits or boundaries. He cannot be measured or compared to any finite standard. Everything within our world is finite, but God, and only God, is infinite. This means that His love for us is infinite, His holiness is infinite, His mercy is infinite—indeed, all of His qualities are unlimited in their scope and expression. This is tough to grasp but absolutely true.

## GOD IS SELF-EXISTENT

Everything in the universe had a beginning, except God. He had no beginning, and He was not created. Because He is the Creator, He is the only One who exists outside of the created order. Again, this is mind boggling but true.

## GOD IS ETERNAL

He is not bound by the dimension of time. He has no end. Before He spoke the first word of creation, time did not exist. He created time as a temporary context for His creation. It really does stretch our minds to realize that God experiences all past, present, and future events simultaneously. How can we possibly comprehend that?

*God offers us the privilege of participating with Him in the fulfillment of His purposes.*

With God, everything that has ever happened or will ever happen has already occurred within His awareness. God sees the beginning of the parade of life, and He sees its end. We look at it through a keyhole or a knothole, and all we know is what we see happening within our range of vision. Who can even begin to imagine what it must be like to live outside the boundary of time? All of history is but a flicker within the spectrum of eternity. And God encompasses all of eternity!

## GOD IS SELF-SUFFICIENT

He has no needs and depends upon nothing outside Himself. All of creation relies upon God for existence and for the maintenance of life. But God has no need for anything, and He does not require help in anything. Thankfully, He does offer us the privilege of participating with Him in the fulfillment of His purposes. And though He does not *need* us, He wants us to be involved with Him.

❧

Our glorious God is truly beyond our comprehension in so many ways. We simply will never be able to fully understand His magnificence, certainly not while we are here on earth.

I have often marveled that a God so vast and unimaginable would be willing to step within the boundaries of space and time to become a mere human being, be born of a woman, and live on this planet. It is incredible to think that He was willing to make such a sacrifice because He wanted to give us the opportunity to experience His love and to behold His glory—to help us see Him and know Him, even with our limited minds.

# 4

# God Is Three Persons in One

The Bible describes God as being triune. This means He is one God, but in three different Persons. This is one of the most difficult things for us to understand. Yet this truth is one of the most important aspects of God's relationship with us.

## THE TRINITY

Theologians have called God's threefold nature "the Trinity." The members of the Trinity are involved with everything together, yet they also have distinct roles. This is hinted at in the very first chapter in the Bible: "Let *us* make people in *our* image" (Genesis 1:26). The plural pronouns *us* and *our* mean that more than one person was involved. Who else but God was present during creation? No one. Therefore, the Trinity in its simplest terms means one God manifested in three persons with three distinctive roles.

## GOD THE FATHER

God the Father is the first person of the Trinity. In general, He orchestrates action. For example, He sent to earth God the Son, Jesus, and bestowed His authority upon Him.

## GOD THE SON

God the Son is the second person of the Trinity. Jesus Christ is fully God and fully human. He is the cornerstone and head of the worldwide church. Jesus now sits at the right hand of God the Father, interceding for all believers.

## GOD THE HOLY SPIRIT

God the Holy Spirit, the third person of the Trinity, is our Comforter. As the "active arm" of God on earth, He lives within believers and guides us into all truth. He convicts us of sin and helps us know God and His will.

—————❖—————

*Jesus now sits at the right hand of God the Father, interceding for all believers.*

—————————

Each member of the Trinity has His own role to play, but each is fully God. God is not three separate Gods as some might envision but has complete unity. No person in the Trinity is less important, less powerful, or less of anything than any other members.

Again, all of this is difficult for us to comprehend. Our minds strain to understand how God the Father, God the Son, and God the Holy Spirit can be distinct personalities, coequal, yet one at the same time. Our best efforts to understand this relationship fall far short.

One popular analogy is to compare the Trinity to water. Water can be in three distinct forms: liquid, ice, or steam. The same chemical formula, $H_2O$, can assume each form under different temperatures. In a similar way, God assumes three different "forms" to accomplish His purposes.

Here is another analogy. We all play different roles in our lives. I am a husband, father and grandfather, and the head of an international organization. I perform different duties in each role, yet I am the same person. God also performs different roles—heavenly Father, loving Son, and Spirit of comfort.

> *God performs different roles— heavenly Father, loving Son, and Spirit of comfort.*

Of course, the Trinity is far more complex and profound than any analogies found within our earthly realm, but at least they help us see how one individual or element can fulfill different roles and responsibilities. So it is with our mysterious and magnificent God.

——————◆——————

HOW FAR WILL YOU GO IN TRUSTING HIM?

# 5

# Trusting God Completely

D o you find yourself doubting God when you are faced with a difficult situation? Is it hard for you to trust God with the challenges of life? A proper understanding of God's nature is crucial to being able to trust Him with our problems.

## CAN I REALLY TRUST GOD?

P eople have many different perceptions of what God is like, and this makes it difficult for them to put their total trust in Him. Some see Him as an indulgent grandfather or divine Santa Claus. Others see Him as aloof, indifferent, and uncaring. Still others see Him as critical and judgmental—someone to be feared and avoided.

Sometimes we do not trust God because of negative life experiences that caused us to be untrusting of *anybody*. I am reminded of a trip I took to the Soviet Union in 1978. At the height of the cold war between the Soviet Union and the United States, the Soviet government, at the request of the Russian church, invited me to visit that vast land. During my visit to eight cities, I knew that millions of people were imprisoned by their own fear, all the result of decades of mental and physical abuse. The KGB, the secret police of the Soviet government, used intimidation and coercion to discover any information it could about the activities

*It's possible that you do not have anyone you truly trust with your deepest fears and most powerful longings.*

and views of political dissidents, Christians, and Jews. Under this kind of suspicion and tyranny, no one trusted anyone else. Even family members turned against each other in this oppressive environment. That society did more to damage those people's ability to trust anyone, including God, than we in the West can imagine.

As a result of your personal life journey, you may wonder, *Who can I really trust?* Perhaps you have been terribly disappointed by someone you did trust. Perhaps you had a parent who consistently failed you. Maybe you had a friend or loved one who betrayed you. It's possible that you do not have anyone you truly trust with your deepest fears and most powerful longings.

In many cases, our past experiences, backgrounds, and personalities shape how we view other people and how we develop relationships with them. If someone we trusted hurt us, we hesitate to trust anyone else again. Although trust is an important part of any healthy friendship, building trust can be extremely difficult.

But what about God? Can He be trusted? How far will you go in trusting Him? What experiences have you had that make it difficult for you to trust even God? The only way to overcome this lack of trust is to deeply understand who He is—the kind of loving, compassionate God He really is. Only then will you be able to trust Him completely.

## HOW TO TRUST

Suppose you needed a ride home from a party late at night, and someone said, "Hey, I'll take you." You would quickly assess whether you could or could not trust the person. First, you would consider that person's ability: Does he have a car and a driver's license? Next you would look at that person's integrity: Will he follow through and do what he said he would? And then you would question his commitment to you: Will he forget about you if something else comes along or if it suddenly becomes inconvenient for him?

Questions such as these usually go through our heads when we are evaluating someone's trustworthi-

*Scripture is clear that God has absolutely unlimited abilities. Nothing is beyond His reach.*

ness. So let us look at God in the same way: Is He able? Does He have integrity? And is He committed to you?

God is able to do whatever you need—or might some things be beyond Him? Well, Scripture is clear that He has absolutely unlimited abilities. He can do *anything*. He is sovereign, all-powerful, ever-present, and all-knowing. Nothing is too difficult for Him. Nothing is beyond His reach.

## "BECAUSE GOD"

I have developed thirteen "Because God" statements (see appendix A) that pertain to His attributes. The first is "Because God is a personal Spirit, you can seek intimate fellowship with Him." The next four address the fact of God's ability:

- Because God is all-powerful, He can help you with anything.
- Because God is ever-present, He is always with you.
- Because God knows everything, you can go to Him with all your questions and concerns.
- Because God is sovereign, He expects you to joyfully submit to His will.

God is definitely able to do whatever you need. However, does He have integrity so you can count on Him to do what He promises? Scripture makes it clear that God's character is of the highest integrity imaginable. He is morally perfect in every way, so He will always do the right thing. He is holy, absolutely truthful, righteous, and just. He will never betray your confidence. My next four "Because God" statements summarize His attributes of integrity:

*Because God is totally committed to His relationship with you, He will always do what is best for you.*

- Because God is holy, you can devote yourself to Him in purity, worship, and service.
- Because God is absolute truth, you can believe what He says and live accordingly.
- Because God is righteous, you can live by His standards.
- Because God is just, you can be sure He will always treat you fairly.

Finally, is God committed to you? Scripture is clear on this point as well. He is utterly committed to you; in fact, God is infinitely more concerned about your well-being than you are. He is totally committed to His relationship with you, so you can experience the many blessings of His grace and goodness.

He is loving, merciful, faithful, and reliable. He will always do what is best for you.

My final four "Because God" statements summarize the relationship attributes of God:

- Because God is love, He is unconditionally committed to your well-being.
- Because God is merciful, He forgives you of your sins when you sincerely confess them.
- Because God is faithful, you can trust Him to always keep His promises.
- Because God never changes, your future is secure and eternal.

In the next several chapters, we will look at each attribute individually. However, it is important to remember that all of God's attributes are interactive and interrelated. With our human limitations, we dissect God's nature into parts so we can understand them. But that is not how they exist in God's character. Each attribute is perfectly complete and fully part of God's personality.

As we study these attributes, keep in mind that if we exalt one of God's qualities over another, we might develop a distorted view of God's character. In fact, overemphasizing any one of God's attributes to the exclusion of others can lead to heresy. For example, teaching only about God's mercy and neglecting His role as a judge will prevent people from understanding God's hatred of sin and the future punishment for wrongdoing. Therefore, as we study each quality individually, we must remember that it is only one aspect of God's magnificent nature. As you gain deeper insight into God's flawless, magnificent character, your trust in Him will skyrocket. He truly is a God who can be trusted!

———————— ❖ ————————

"Everything I plan will come to pass,
for I will do whatever I wish."

Isaiah 46:10

————————————————

# 6

## God Is All-Powerful

When was the last time you tried to accomplish something completely beyond your ability? Perhaps you have valiantly concentrated all your energy on the challenge at hand only to find that it was not enough to complete the task. Afterward, you felt exhausted and defeated.

God is capable of doing anything—so long as it does not violate His other attributes. (For example, He cannot lie, change, deny Himself, or be tempted.) Otherwise, no task is too large or too difficult for Him.

### OUR POWERFUL GOD

Our Lord never fails or gets tired. Because He is all-powerful, He has the ability and the strength to do whatever He pleases. His power is not restrained or inhibited in any way by His created beings. God generates power within Himself and does what He chooses to do whenever He chooses to do it. He is never tired, frustrated, or discouraged. His power is not an abstract idea, but a force to be reckoned with. Theologians use the term *omnipotence* to describe the awesome, unlimited power of God.

### MORE THAN THE UNIVERSE

To get just a small idea of God's creative power, let us consider our universe. We live on one of nine planets that revolve around the sun. As the dominant light of our solar system, our sun gives off far more energy in one second than all mankind has produced since creation. With a diameter of approximately 860,000 miles, the sun could hold one million planets the size of Earth. Yet our sun is only an average-size star.

Our sun is just one among 100 billion stars in our galaxy, the Milky Way. The Pistol Star gives off ten million times the power generated by our sun, and one million stars the size of our sun can fit easily within its sphere. It takes 100,000 light-years to travel from one side of the Milky Way to the other. Our galaxy is moving through space at a phenomenal speed of one million miles per hour. If the Milky Way were compared to the size of the North American continent, our solar system would be about the size of a coffee cup!

*In all my years as a believer, I have found God faithful to use His power on behalf of those who seek Him.*

Yet our Milky Way is not a huge galaxy. One of our neighboring galaxies, the Andromeda spiral galaxy, is two million light-years away and contains about 400 billion stars. No one knows how many galaxies there are in the universe, but scientists estimate that there are billions of them.

The prophet Isaiah wrote, "Look up into the heavens. Who created all the stars? He brings them out one after another, calling each by its name. And he counts them to see that none are lost or have strayed away" (40:26). Scientists estimate that there are ten billion trillion stars in the universe, or about as many stars as there are grains of sand on all of our planet's seashores. If all the stars were divided equally among the people of the world, each person would receive almost two trillion stars.

God merely spoke, and this unfathomable universe came into being—a universe that astronomers estimate contains more than 100 billion galaxies. But all of the power contained within this entire universe is but a small representation of the unlimited power of God. The combined energy of all of Earth's storms, winds, ocean currents, and other forces of nature do not equal even a fraction of God's almighty power. Truly, God is omnipotent. His power is inherent in His nature. He does not derive His power from any other source; all power has always been His and will continue to be His for eternity. In fact, any power that we have comes ultimately from God.

### MORE THAN ALL THE NATIONS

Consider, too, that God is more powerful than all the rulers on earth. Do the nuclear capabilities, chemical weapons, and military strength of other countries frighten you? We do not need to fear. Isaiah wrote, "All the nations of the world are nothing in comparison with him. They are but a drop in the bucket, dust on the scales" (40:15). After learning firsthand of God's power, King Nebuchadnezzar acknowledged, "He does as he pleases with the powers of heaven and the peoples of the earth. No one can hold back his hand or say to him: 'What have you done?'" (Daniel 4:35 NIV).

We need not fear that any one person or nation will put God to the test. He is so far above earthly governments that they can do nothing outside His power. No ruler or army can change any plan that God has made. When we study God's Word from Genesis to Revelation, we get a glimpse of how He directs history and nations. Although events at times make no sense to us, God knows the end from the beginning and has us in the palm of His hand.

## More than Satan

God is also infinitely more powerful than Satan and his evil legions. God is not intimidated by the Devil's rebellious hatred. God is the Creator; Satan is a created being who can operate only within the prescribed limits God places on him. Satan is nothing compared to God. Romans 16:20 gives this promise: "The God of peace will soon crush Satan under your feet." How encouraging that promise is when we are battling the evil forces that confront us every day!

Whatever God chooses will come to pass because He has the omnipotent ability to make it happen. God told Isaiah, "Everything I plan will come to pass, for I will do whatever I wish" (46:10). Speaking to God, Job acknowledged, "I know that you can do all things; no plan of yours can be thwarted" (Job 42:2 NIV). Because God is all-powerful, He has the ability and the strength to do whatever He pleases. His power is not restrained or inhibited by any of His created beings.

## God's Plan for You

Perhaps you have asked yourself: *How much can I expect God to do through me? How involved is He in what I see going on around me? What is He willing to accomplish in my life?* Many people are skeptical about God's willingness to become intimately involved in their affairs. They may agree that God has a general purpose for everything, but they wonder if God even knows or cares about the details in their lives.

In His Word, however, God declares that He has a plan for this world and every person in it: "I have a plan for the whole earth, for my mighty power reaches throughout the world" (Isaiah 14:26). No matter what happens anywhere in the world at any moment, God is always in control. Sometimes this world seems chaotic and out of control, yet God knows what is in the future. God has unlimited power within himself and does what He wants with it. This would be terrifying if God were a tyrant who meted out His power indiscriminately. Fortunately, the Bible says God acts out of love and righteousness (attributes we will examine later).

Some of us may question why God does not answer our prayers when we ask Him for things. But God is not a "genie" or Santa Claus who gives us everything we ask for just the way we want it. He uses His power to fulfill His purposes, plans, and will for us and everyone involved in our situations. He knows what we need far better than we do. Can you think of at least one prayer request for which you are now thankful God did not answer the way you wanted? Often we pray selfishly or from our fleshly

*Our all-powerful Creator cares for us, and He longs to exhibit His power in our lives.*

nature. But as we align our ways and desires with His perfect will and pray in faith, we will see His power displayed more frequently in answered prayer.

The apostle Paul tells us that God demonstrates His power through His Son (see 1 Corinthians 1:24). We can see evidence of this in His virgin birth. God planned before the foundation of the world to send His Son to die for us. God's ultimate display of power was raising Jesus Christ from the dead. After Jesus' death by crucifixion, His enemies put a Roman seal on the tomb and set guards to make sure no one disturbed His body. Yet their efforts meant nothing to God. When He was ready to show His power, He simply rolled the stone away from the tomb, and Jesus walked out alive and well.

Our all-powerful Creator cares for us, and He longs to exhibit His power in our lives. Indeed, Paul writes that the power available to us as believers is "the same mighty power that raised Christ from the dead and seated him in the place of honor at God's right hand in the heavenly realms" (Ephesians 1:19–20). The amount of power available to us through God's Spirit is equal to the power God used to raise Christ from the dead! Like Paul, we can honestly say, "I can do everything with the help of Christ who gives me the strength I need" (Philippians 4:13).

> *No matter what you might be facing, God can help you. Nothing is too hard for Him.*

No matter what you might be facing, God can help you. Nothing is too hard for Him. There is not a need too great for Him to meet. There is not a problem too complicated for Him to solve. There is not a foe too strong for Him to conquer. There is not a prayer too difficult for Him to answer. The Bible promises, "[God] is able to do immeasurably more than all we ask or imagine, according to his power that is at work within us" (Ephesians 3:20 NIV).

As we begin to understand our God's vast and magnificent power, our lives cannot help but be transformed. Everything about us will change—our attitudes, actions, motives, desires, lifestyle, and even our view of God. As we are transformed, we light up the world around us. Our society—which was once darkened by fear, ignorance, and hopelessness—will become lightened with our witness of God's power, care, and intervention in our lives.

In all my years as a believer, I have found God faithful to use His power on behalf of those who seek Him. A right understanding of who God is will revolutionize the life of every believer. It will launch you into the exciting adventure of supernatural living in the power of this mighty God. Because God is all-powerful, He can help you with anything.

---❖---

"FOR IN HIM WE LIVE AND MOVE AND EXIST."

ACTS 17:28

---

# 7

# God Is Ever-Present

God is present everywhere at the same time. His ability to be all places at all times is called *omnipresence*. This means there is not a sliver of space anywhere in the universe that He does not dynamically and powerfully occupy. Everywhere throughout the world, God is always and immediately present with all of who He is! He is not limited by a body; He is a Spirit who moves wherever He wishes.

## GOD IS EVERYWHERE

How can we explain His Spirit presence? Many writers have compared it to the wind. No one can box it in or stop it from blowing. No one can see the wind; it comes and goes as it pleases. Yet we can see the results of wind. We see its massive force in rolling tornadoes, hurricanes, and typhoons. The wind can also be gentle, like the whisper of a breeze off the ocean. It can bring the smell of soft rain on the leaves or the freshness of spring through an open window. Is this not like the amazing breadth of our God, who can both topple rulers and calm the fears of a little child?

The wind analogy, however, is inadequate to completely describe the awesome presence of our infinite Creator. His power does not sweep over a particular area and then move on to some other place. Unlike the wind, He is everywhere at the same time. Not a single atom in any galaxy is hidden from His sight.

Many religions believe that God's existence is somehow bound up with His creation. The belief that God is everything and everything is God is called *pantheism*. Hindus, for instance, believe that if you touch a tree, you touch God. To carry it further, this belief leads to the conclusion that since everything is god, *we* are gods.

————————❖————————

*God's magnificent presence is all we need for any challenge that may come our way.*

————————————————

But pantheism is not what the Bible means when it describes God's omnipresence. Author and pastor Bill Hybels explains the difference this way:

> The Bible says that God is Spirit, so technically, He doesn't dwell in three-dimensional space as we do (John 15:15). His *presence* is everywhere, but not His *essence* (that would be the heresy known as pantheism). God is no less present in one portion of the universe than any other. And He is no more present anywhere than where you are right now. In other words, anyone, anywhere in the universe might say, "The Lord is in this place." Wherever you are, God is right there, right now. [1]

Although God is distinct from His creation, all of His creation exists within Him. As the apostle Paul said, "For in him we live and move and exist" (Acts 17:28). We live in His glorious presence every moment of every day. When we are by ourselves, God watches what we do. When we privately do something good that nobody else knows about, God still sees it and will reward us accordingly. He also sees the bad things we do in secret. The Bible states, "Nothing in all creation can hide from him. Everything is naked and exposed before his eyes. This is the God to

*God walks with us, gives us strength, and understands our pain.*

whom we must explain all that we have done" (Hebrews 4:13).

God is not just watching us from afar; we actually have His Spirit living inside us. The apostle Paul wrote, "Don't you realize that all of you together are the temple of God and that the Spirit of God lives in you?" (1 Corinthians 3:16).

Our confidence is in the ever-present nature of God. We can be sure that He sees us, walks with us, and loves us no matter where we are. God's omnipresence means that we cannot go anywhere that God is not beside us. As the psalmist wrote, "If I go up to the heavens, you are there; if I make my bed in the depths, you are there. If I rise on the wings of the dawn, if I settle on the far side of the sea, even there your hand will guide me, your right hand will hold me fast" (139:8–10 NIV).

Have you had an experience that left you wondering where God is? Sometimes we do not feel God's presence, but emotions can be misleading. No matter what we feel, God is still there. No matter what the situation, He is still beside us. What crisis are you facing right now? Unemployment, serious health problems, the breakup of your marriage, rebellious teenage children, rejection by those who once loved you? God walks with us, gives us strength, understands our pain, and knows how to handle our problems. He will help us if we only ask Him and are willing to do things His way and in His time. Isaiah 43:1–3 records God's precious promise to be with us in times of crisis:

> The LORD who created you says: "Do not be afraid, for I have ransomed you. I have called you by name; you are mine. When you go through deep waters and great trouble, I will be with you. When you go through rivers of difficulty, you will not drown! When you walk through the fire of oppression, you will not be burned up; the flames will not consume you. For I am the LORD, your God, the Holy One of Israel, your Savior."

Living in God's presence means realizing that He is with you and is vitally concerned about *every* part of your life. Consider what God's participation in our lives means:

When we are confused, God will guide us.
When we are afraid, God will protect us.
When we are tempted, God will help us resist.
When we are hurting, God will comfort us.
When we are discouraged, God will encourage us.
When we are lonely, God will be our companion.

No person or circumstance can ever remove us from the presence of our loving God. Paul writes, "I am convinced that nothing can ever separate us from his love. Death can't, and life can't. The angels can't, and the demons can't. Our fears for today, our worries about tomorrow, and even the powers of hell can't keep God's love away. Whether we are high above the sky or in the deepest ocean, nothing in all creation will ever be able to separate us from the love of God that is revealed in Christ Jesus our Lord" (Romans 8:38–39).

## God Knows Everything

What a person knows can lead to riches, power, and advancement. Major corporations and companies pay consultants handsomely for what they know. Consider the computer industry. Fortunes are being made because people want quicker ways to find and manage information.

Yet the more we learn, the more we realize how much we still do not know. To compensate for our lack of knowledge, we

> ❖
>
> *Only the Lord knows us perfectly and intimately. He understands our desires, motives, and thoughts.*

are always trying to develop faster, more efficient ways to access knowledge. Most scientists spend their lives trying to understand and solve the mysteries of life and the universe. But for our all-knowing God, there are no mysteries. He has a clear understanding of everything that baffles mankind.

### God Is Omniscient

God knows the answers to all of life's questions. Unlike us, He is never surprised or bewildered because He is completely aware of all events past, present, and future. Our magnificent Creator knows everything and is the source of all true knowledge, understanding, and wisdom. His knowledge is undefiled by any distortions or wrong perspectives. It is always totally true and accurate.

Theologians call God's unlimited knowledge *omniscience* (all-knowing). What does God's omniscience mean? Because

God knows absolutely everything that can ever be known, He has never had to learn anything. He does not need a computer, because all knowledge is instantly accessible to Him and He remembers everything at all times. He never has to figure something out; everything is always absolutely clear to Him. Nothing ever turns out differently from what He expected or planned. In the book of Isaiah, God declares, "I am God, and there is no one else like me. Only I can tell you what is going to happen even before it happens" (46:9–10).

*There is neither a thought in your mind nor a motive in your heart that God does not know.*

God's omniscience is vitally important to us. As we get to know Him more intimately, we realize that we can trust Him because He does know everything we have done and will do— yet He loves us anyway. There is neither a thought in your mind nor a motive in your heart that God does not know. As King David explained:

> O LORD, you have examined my heart and know everything about me. You know when I sit down or stand up. You know my every thought when far away. You chart the path ahead of me and tell me where to stop and rest. Every moment you know where I am. You know what I am going to say even before I say it, LORD. You both precede and follow me. You place your hand of blessing on my head. Such knowledge is too wonderful for me, too great for me to know!
>
> PSALM 139:1–6

## GOD LOVES UNCONDITIONALLY

Some people are intimidated by God because He knows the end from the beginning—and everything in between. Statements such as Proverbs 15:3 unnerve them: "The LORD is watching everywhere, keeping his eye on both the evil and the good." These people know that God sees their sin. On the other hand, God's omniscience is comforting to those who confess their sins as they recognize them. They know their sins have been forgiven.

God loves you unconditionally. He will forgive you when you sincerely confess your sin to Him. We never have to fear that He will discover something in our lives that will change His mind about loving us. Only the Lord knows us perfectly and intimately. He understands our desires, motives, and thoughts. Nothing about us escapes His notice. In fact, God knows infinitely more about us than we will ever know about ourselves.

*As our Creator, God custom-designed us for a unique purpose.*

Do you ever feel that your parents do not listen to you, that your boss does not respect you, or that your friends do not understand you? How devastating to realize that almost no one knows what you are like inside or the dreams you hold dear. Take heart. Remember that God knows how we are formed. As our Creator, He custom-designed us for a unique purpose.

## GOD UNDERSTANDS

When you face challenges or difficulties, you can be encouraged that God understands what you are going through. Your feelings and struggles are not unknown to Him, but He also knows the purposes for your trials. He wants to help you accomplish those purposes and experience His joy through them. In fact, God gave us this promise: "For I know the plans I have for you … plans for good and not for disaster, to give you a future and a hope" (Jeremiah 29:11).

God understands our capabilities, opportunities, and life mission. We can trust Him with every moment of our future. The apostle Paul wrote, "Oh, what a wonderful God we have! How great are his riches and wisdom and knowledge! How impossible it is for us to understand his decisions and his methods! For who can know what the Lord is thinking? Who knows enough to be his counselor?" (Romans 11:33–34).

## OUR TEACHER, COUNSELOR, GUIDE

Unfortunately, sometimes we think we know better than God does and do not listen to Him. How many times have you gotten impatient with the way your life is going and wanted to go directly from point A to point C? But it is not just getting to the destination that is important. God knows that by taking us through point B, the process of the journey will change us into the kind of people we need to be when we arrive at our destination. Following His plan leads to the best choices for our lives—right now, in the future, and for eternity.

> *We can trust God because He does know everything we have done and will do—yet He loves us anyway.*

Because God's Spirit resides within us, we can rely on Him as our Teacher, Counselor, and Guide into all truth. He is willing to share His great knowledge with us. But we often deprive ourselves of God's solutions because we do not take time to study His Word. Or we may know the Word but do not obey it or meet the conditions of

God's promises. And so we do not receive full benefit from God's omniscience.

God even understands our temptations. He tells us in the Bible, "No temptation has seized you except what is common to man. And God is faithful; he will not let you be tempted beyond what you can bear. But when you are tempted, he will also provide a way out so that you can stand up under it" (1 Corinthians 10:13 NIV). We sometimes wish we knew what that way out would be. Yet we can rest assured that the God who knows the end from the beginning is providing the way out. He has the power to make us victorious.

Open your heart to God, and determine to walk with Him regardless of the cost. Remind yourself every day of the promises of our all-knowing God. You will never again feel the same about your daily personal fellowship with our wonderful God. As James wrote, "If any of you lacks wisdom, he should ask of God, who gives generously to all without finding fault, and it will be given to him. But when he asks, he must believe and not doubt, because he who doubts is like a wave of the sea, blown and tossed by the wind. That man should not think he will receive anything from the Lord" (1:5–7 NIV). Because God knows everything, you can go to Him with all your questions and concerns.

---

1. Bill Hybels, *The God You're Looking For* (Nashville, Tenn.: Thomas Nelson, 1997), p. 24.

―――――――❖―――――――

"HE DETERMINES THE COURSE OF WORLD EVENTS; HE
REMOVES KINGS AND SETS OTHERS ON THE THRONE."

DANIEL 2:21

―――――――――

# 8

# God Is Sovereign

As members of a democratic society rife with individualism, Americans have difficulty understanding God as an absolute ruler. Did we not reject living under a sovereign ruler when the American Colonies revolted against the king of England? Why should we be subject to anyone now? Yes, we Americans love our independence and freedom.

With the decline in the belief in absolute truth, we tend to argue and debate our points of view with everyone, even our leaders. Today we negotiate to get our own way and advance our agendas. Compromise—even on moral issues—is considered a virtue. But we cannot argue, debate, or negotiate with God, the King of the universe. If He is truly the Lord of our lives and we are His true disciples, we say, "Yes, Lord!" Indeed, saying, "No, Lord," would be a contradiction of terms for the true disciple of Jesus Christ.

## GOD IS KING

From earliest days, kings and queens have received honor and respect. Yet there exists a King whose majesty, splendor, and awesomeness are almost indescribable. Compared to Him, no other ruler or reigning power is even a blip on the screen of eternity. He does not need ceremony or grandeur to appear more regal. Jewels and wealth mean nothing to Him. Yes, this divine Ruler, our sovereign God, has His throne far above the universe in heaven.

David, himself a king, asked, "Who is the King of glory?" Then he answers his own question: "The LORD, strong and mighty, the LORD, invincible in battle.... The LORD Almighty—he is the King of glory" (Psalm 24:8–10).

The throne of an earthly king or queen, however grand it may be, cannot compare to the glories of God. If we took away the royal trappings from any human ruler, the person would look just like one of us. Honor is derived from ceremonies and the homage paid by other people. The sovereign may have the power of an army, but behind the marks of authority is a sinful, imperfect human being just like you and me.

God's reign is different. God does not derive His right to rule from anyone or anything. No title was bestowed on Him by another person, and there is no higher authority any-where. The great I AM always does what He knows is best and answers to no one. His reign is so magnificent that we cannot even comprehend it. He is the sovereign Ruler of the universe. King David proclaimed, "Yours, O LORD, is the kingdom; you are exalted as head over all. Wealth and honor come from you; you are the ruler of all things. In your hands are strength and power to exalt and give strength to all" (1 Chronicles 29:11–12 NIV).

God has power to do anything that needs to be done. He is present everywhere, so no one can hide from Him or escape His scrutiny. He is all-knowing, so there is nothing about which

He is unaware. Amazingly, this great God loves you and me unconditionally, caring for the smallest need of the least of us.

## God's Plan for Us

Submitting to God's sovereignty can be compared to putting together a billion-piece puzzle. History is like that giant picture. Only by looking at the photograph on the box cover could you determine what everything will look like once all the pieces are in place. Now imagine that you are given one piece of the puzzle. This represents where you fit into God's master plan. What can you do with this piece? You have never seen the picture on the outside of the box. All you know is that your piece has a little dark color here and a few bright spots there.

> *If you let God direct you, He will help you find your place within His grand plan.*

From a human standpoint, it is impossible to understand the master plan—how everything fits together. But if you let God direct you, He will help you find your place within His grand plan. He is not only big enough to see the whole picture, but He is the One who created it.

We can see part of God's overall picture by reading the Bible. God gives us clues as to what His purposes are for us. In His sovereignty, He will fulfill all He has promised in His Word. God reigns so supremely above His creation that we cannot question any of His actions. Whatever God wants to have happen will happen; His will cannot be thwarted. As the prophet Daniel said, "He determines the course of world events; he removes kings and sets others on the throne" (2:21). Nothing occurs without His divine permission.

God commands the forces of nature and uses them to achieve His divine purposes. He established the scientific laws that regulate the universe, and only He can overrule their effect. For God, miracles are "routine." I am amazed when I hear from Christians who doubt God's supernatural intervention in their lives. God did mighty miracles through Noah, Moses, and other Old Testament char-

---❖---

*Understanding God's power and authority causes us to focus on Him, not ourselves.*

---

acters. He spoke through the prophets. He personally entered our time and space in the form of His Son, the Lord Jesus Christ. Jesus performed miracles, died for our sins, rose from the grave, and ascended bodily into heaven. His resurrection was the greatest miracle of all. Even today, God is in the business of turning tragedy into triumph and sorrow into joy.

God actively directs His creation toward a predetermined conclusion. However, we do not live under the jurisdiction of a dictatorial ruler who deprives us of all the fun and happiness. The King of kings and Lord of lords has our best interest at heart at all times. He orchestrates events to enable us to praise Him and glorify His name.

Part of our problem with accepting God's authority is that we have lost our concept of majesty. With little sense of the magnificence of God, we have trouble submitting to His sovereignty and worshiping Him.

## GOD'S PURPOSE FOR US

Understanding God's power and authority causes us to focus on Him, not ourselves. Our response is to fall at His feet and give Him everything we are and own. We cannot force God to do things our way. Sometimes in His wisdom and sovereign plan, His answer to our prayers is "no" or "wait." Our position is to trust, believe, and obey, not to demand.

Does that mean we have no say with our sovereign God? Of course not! He does not consider us His puppets or slaves. He made us as free moral agents with minds, wills, and emotions. He will not force His love and plans upon us against our wills. Within the context of His master plan, God gives us the freedom to choose.

This is a hard concept to grasp, but think of it this way: When I flew to Dallas a few days ago, I had complete freedom to get up and walk around inside the aircraft. I could go get a magazine or talk to my fellow passengers. I could take a nap or make a telephone call. I had complete freedom—within limits. I could not, however, alter the airplane's course. That plane was going to Dallas!

Our relationship with God is like that. We are not robots mechanically programmed to follow His decrees. God has a course for us that has been charted before the beginning of time. God assures us in His Word, "My purpose will stand, and I will do all that I please" (Isaiah 46:10 NIV).

*No event escapes His notice. No person is beyond His influence. No circumstance exists outside His control.*

His master plan for history will be accomplished, whether we choose to work with Him or go our own stubborn way. Although He allows us to choose and suffer the consequences of our choices, He never relinquishes control of the plans to accomplish His purposes. God turns the pages of history; we do not.

The next time you feel overwhelmed by life challenges and setbacks, remember that your loving God is still in control. He is sovereignly directing your life. The book of Proverbs states, "Many are the plans in a man's heart, but it is the LORD's purpose that prevails" (19:21 NIV). God carefully supervises all that happens. No event escapes His notice. No person is beyond His influence. No circumstance exists outside His control.

You may have wondered, *If God is in complete control of everything, why does He allow birth defects, famines, and war? Why does He permit sin, evil, and suffering?* God's very nature opposes these things. It was not His plan for Adam and Eve to sin and bring sickness, disease, and death upon mankind. God created a perfect world, but man chose to sin, and the penalty for sin was death—physical and spiritual. This curse of death has affected all of creation, not just humans. All the bad things that happen are due to living in a world under judgment, a fallen world. Part of Adam and Eve's punishment was pain and suffering in childbirth, toiling for food, and struggling to make a living.

> *God is far more concerned about the quality of our eternal future than He is about our present comfort.*

God does not initiate, cause, or authorize sin. Nor does He tempt anyone to sin. Yet He tolerates evil for a season to fulfill His righteous plans for people to respond by their own free will to His love. Pastor Charles Stanley explains that God allows troubles, accidents, adversity, and similar problems to come into our lives for a purpose. Some of these purposes are:

To get our attention
To draw us to Himself
To help us get to know Him
To see Him as He is
To taste of His goodness

To have an intimate, close relationship with Him

To prevent distance from and avoidance of God[1]

God is far more concerned about the quality of our eternal future than He is about our present comfort. In fact, difficulties and suffering are tools with which He shapes us into the image of Jesus Christ. It is never pleasant to be enrolled in the school of hard knocks, the academy of adversity. But unless God takes us through the curriculum of trials, we will never become the quality people He wants us to be. Adversity is the touchstone of character.

God uses even the most disastrous situations for our good. As Romans 8:28 promises, "God causes everything to work together for the good of those who love God and are called according to his purpose for them." We can give all our worries to God, knowing that He cares about what happens to us. When tragedy strikes, take comfort in the fact that no difficulty will ever come into your life without God's permission. Knowing this truth does not make adversity easy, but it gives us hope that the result will be worth whatever pain we endure.

I urge you to allow God to direct your life by surrendering your decisions, trials, hurts, and pain to Him. Give Him your joys, accomplishments, and treasures. Unlike an earthly king, God will take what we give to Him and multiply blessings in our lives. We do not give up anything but pride, sin, and temporal possessions; He gives us back eternal life, joy, spiritual riches, and an eternal reign with Him! Because God is sovereign, He expects you to submit to His will.

---

1. Charles Stanley, "Where Our Needs Are Met" audiocassette, InTouch Ministries, Atlanta, Georgia.

———————— ❖ ————————

"WHO ELSE AMONG THE GODS IS LIKE YOU, O LORD? WHO
IS GLORIOUS IN HOLINESS LIKE YOU—SO AWESOME IN
SPLENDOR, PERFORMING SUCH WONDERS?"

EXODUS 15:11

————————————————

# 9

# God Is Holy

Have you ever known anyone who was extremely talented but morally flawed? It does not take long to realize that great ability without solid character can cause immense tragedy and grief. An individual's character, rather than his abilities, determines the lasting value of his accomplishments.

For example, the president of a famous university was discovered using his computer to transfer pornographic material to minors. The head of a prestigious charitable organization was convicted of embezzling. Several top political leaders have been accused of committing adultery with interns and staff. Obviously, not all people in high-profile professions are guilty of such offenses, but problems such as these are so rampant that moral degradation has become commonplace.

Christians also struggle with moral purity. Some time ago, a man who held an influential position in a Christian ministry confided in me that he had never surrendered his life to Christ, although for years he pretended that he had done so. He said and did all the right things so that his

# BILL BRIGHT

friends and all who met him would think he was a committed follower of Christ. But he admitted to deliberately rejecting the Holy Spirit's leading.

I was shocked that anyone who was exposed to the inspired Word of God, Christian fellowship, and ministry would dare to flagrantly disobey God. But as we talked, I learned that he was simply afraid to live a holy life. The thought of complete surrender to the Lord was unappealing to him, and as a result, he had run from God for many years.

## LIVING A HOLY LIFE

Like this man, many Christians fail to surrender to God because of a false view of holiness. They have a distorted view of holiness because they define it from a secular viewpoint. They imagine a holy person as some kind of religious fanatic, a "kook," or an isolated monk devoted only to prayer and fasting. Others think that holiness has only to do with the way a person dresses or socializes. These misinformed believers decide they do not want to give up their lifestyle, pleasures, and pride. They do not let God mold them into people with tastes and desires that bring true happiness and joy in fellowship with Him.

> *This is the secret: We can live a holy life if we yield to the Holy Spirit, who came to glorify Jesus Christ.*

It is tragic that some believers continue to wrestle with their childhood experiences with strict, legalistic parents or churches. I have heard some confess, "I tried to live up to the high expectations of my parents or pastor, but I have failed many times. I just can't live the Christian life!" These people conclude that the Christian life is difficult to live. I agree. In

68

fact, I go one step further: It is *impossible* to live a holy life on your own. Even with determination and our best efforts, we will always fail. We can never become holy in our own strength and abilities. We can be thankful that the story does not end with our feeble efforts. Listen to the apostle Paul:

> There is no condemnation for those who belong to Christ Jesus. For the power of the life-giving Spirit has freed you through Christ Jesus from the power of sin that leads to death. The law of Moses could not save us, because of our sinful nature. But God put into effect a different plan to save us. He sent his own Son in a human body like ours, except that ours are sinful. God destroyed sin's control over us by giving his Son as a sacrifice for our sins. He did this so that the requirement of the law would be fully accomplished for us who no longer follow our sinful nature but instead follow the Spirit.
>
> ROMANS 8:1–4

This is the secret: We can live a holy life if we yield to the Holy Spirit, who came to glorify Jesus Christ. Jesus is the only person to ever live a holy life, and now He resides within every believer through His Holy Spirit. His presence and power give us the strength to live a holy life moment by moment.

## THE SECRET TO JOY

Holy, righteous living is the secret to a life of joy, power, victory, and fruitfulness. When we are holy, we are set apart and separated from sin for God's special use. God gives us the power to experience a whole new life based on His holiness and purity. But we must obey His direction and laws.

In 1996, I was privileged to receive the prestigious international Templeton Prize for Progress in Religion. As part of the honor, Vonette and I went to Buckingham Palace to meet with Prince Philip and Sir John Templeton. Because we were meeting royalty, we were very conscious of our appearance and our behavior. We wondered, *What's proper protocol? Are we dressed appropriately? How should we respond?*

> *When we concentrate on God's holiness, the only appropriate response is adoration and reverential respect.*

Do we have less concern when we come before our sovereign God, the Ruler of the universe? He deserves much more reverence and respect than any human being who ever lived! He is not a "supreme being." He is not the "man upstairs." He is the great, holy, righteous, all-powerful, loving Creator God.

Our God is holy. His character is perfect in every way. His moral excellence is the absolute standard of integrity and ethical purity. God's supreme holiness infinitely sets Him apart from His creation. Moses expressed it this way: "Who else among the gods is like you, O Lord? Who is glorious in holiness like you—so awesome in splendor, performing such wonders?" (Exodus 15:11).

As we meditate on God's supreme holiness, we cannot help but be overcome with a sense of awe. The psalmist tells us, "Worship the LORD in the splendor of His holiness; tremble before Him, all the earth" (96:9 NIV). When we concentrate on God's holiness, the only appropriate response is adoration and reverential respect.

Many Scripture passages tell us to fear God. King David

writes, "Serve the LORD with reverent fear, and rejoice with trembling" (Psalm 2:11). Solomon explains, "Fear of the LORD is the beginning of wisdom. Knowledge of the Holy One results in understanding" (Proverbs 9:10). To fear God does not mean to be *afraid* of Him, but to *revere* Him for His magnificent greatness and unlimited authority.

## SET APART FOR HOLINESS

We have been set apart by God to be holy. Rather than reflecting the opinions and attitudes of this sinful world, we are to reflect the beauty of His holiness. But we can only be holy by placing our faith in Jesus Christ. And as the holiness of God works into the fabric of our being, we will become sensitive to sin and learn to abhor it as God does.

God created the universe to function according to His standard of holiness. God's holiness is so complete that He cannot look on even one sin. Picture God's holiness in this way: Envision a beautiful bride on her wedding day, dressed in white and looking radiant. The white dress symbolizes purity. It does not have a spot or wrinkle anywhere. If one noticeable spot stained the dress, people would focus on that blemish rather than the loveliness of the dress. That is a picture of God's purity. God, who has never sinned in any way, is so pure and holy that He "cannot tolerate the slightest sin" (Psalm 5:4). His heaven is pure and holy, absolutely free of all sin and evil.

No matter how religious, self-disciplined, or good we may try to be, we cannot expect God to allow us into His heaven when we have sin stains in our lives. If God allowed one sin to mar His pure dwelling place, it would cease to be a holy city. Since God cannot even look on sin, our sinful, human situation seems hopeless.

This is where a miraculous paradox comes in. Jesus Christ came to take away the sins of the world. The perfect, holy Son of God took on the stain of our sin. He endured and satisfied the judgment of a pure God for our misdeeds—not just one or two sins, but *every* sin you and I have ever committed or will commit in our lifetimes!

Of course, living a pure life is possible only through the enabling of the Holy Spirit. We are given power over sin and temptation as we are filled and anointed by Him. According to God's Word, we do not have to sin. But if we do sin, there is someone to plead for us before the Father. This is what John wrote: "My dear children, I am writing this to you so that you will not sin. But if you do sin, there is someone to plead for you before the Father. He is Jesus Christ, the one who pleases God completely. He is the sacrifice for our sins. He takes away not only our sins but the sins of all the world" (1 John 2:1–2).

Becoming holy is more than obedience; it is a liberating, cleansing freedom from all unwholesomeness. Sin in our lives creates a barrier to fellowship with God. It blocks the communication lines between God and us. Restored fellowship with God comes by confessing our sin and turning from it. As the holiness of God is absorbed into every fiber of our being, we become even more sensitive to sin and learn to abhor it all the more as we walk in an intimate, joyful relationship with Him.

Scripture gives us God's directive: "Now you must be holy in everything you do, just as God—who chose you to be his children—is holy" (1 Peter 1:15). Christians have been set apart by God for this divine purpose. If you want to see the holiness of God, examine the life and teachings of Jesus Christ. He is the visible expression of God's holiness. God wants us to place our lives under His lordship and conform to the moral character of His Son and reflect the beauty of His holiness and character.

Out of respect for God, I want to be holy as He is holy and never disappoint Him in any way. Everyone I know who has been greatly used by God has gone through an experience of "dying to self" as described in Galatians 2:20. It is not until we know the reality of "death to self" that we can live for Christ and God can truly use and bless us.

> *Holy living involves a daily decision to surrender to the lordship of Christ.*

Holy living involves a daily decision to surrender to the lordship of Christ. It involves yielding our will to God and adopting His perspective for life. God wants our minds and hearts to be filled with His holy qualities. As our lives are transformed, we will project the light of His holiness into the darkness of our evil world. Real life—abundant life—begins with dying to self.

## BEWARE THE SUBSTITUTE GODS

Our holy God is jealous of our affections and devotion. He warned the Israelites, "Do not worship any other gods besides me. Do not make idols of any kind … You must never worship or bow down to them, for I, the LORD your God, am a jealous God who will not share your affection with any other god!" (Exodus 20:3–5). He alone has the right to occupy the throne of our heart. He is to be exalted to the highest place in our lives. Everything else must be of lower importance.

Yet we are all guilty at one time or another of idolatry. The false gods and idols of our society may not be as obvious as those of ancient Israel or other cultures, but their presence is just as real. They clamor for our attention. They bargain for our allegiance.

First, much of today's society worships the god of affluence. Many people are convinced that wealth is the key to happiness. They place their trust in bank accounts and hoarded assets. The spirit of greed has gradually transformed their values so that money is their master.

Others turn to the god of pleasure. Multitudes are convinced that fun is the chief goal in life. Couch potatoes vegetate in front of the TV screen. Sports fanatics cannot watch enough games. Some seek entertainment, thrills, and adventure in hopes of conquering boredom in their futile search for happiness.

The ambitious sacrifice themselves to the god of achievement. Pride is their relentless taskmaster. For these workaholics, accomplishments are the building blocks of self-esteem. No challenge is too great in their quest for significance.

Because of the god of infatuation, some people idolize a celebrity, hero, friend, or even a relative. Their entire world revolves around that individual. The spirit of obsession amplifies healthy feelings of love and admiration into unholy worship.

The god of self-worship convinces people that appearance is everything. Their life is preoccupied with beauty, fashion, and bodybuilding.

Finally, the god of sensuality has ensnared many with immorality. For them, God's gift of sex has been distorted into perversion and, tragically, often ends in addiction, abortion, disease, and death.

Substitute gods usurp the worship and devotion that rightfully belong to our holy God. In reality, these idols can never fill the God-shaped vacuum within the heart of man. God's holiness demands your devotion. The apostle John strongly warned, "Dear children, keep away from anything that might take God's place in your hearts" (1 John 5:21). Where is your heart? Are you remaining pure and faithful to your holy God? Because God is holy, you can devote yourself to Him in purity, worship, and service.

"I AM THE WAY, THE TRUTH, AND THE LIFE. NO ONE CAN COME TO THE FATHER EXCEPT THROUGH ME."

—JESUS CHRIST

# 10

# God Is Absolute Truth

A story is told about a banquet speaker who was introduced as a shrewd and smart businessman. His business of growing and selling potatoes in Maine netted him $25,000 the previous year. After a long and glowing introduction, he arose to speak.

"Before I begin," he said, "I must set the record straight. What was said about my business is only partially true. First, it was not Maine, but Texas. It was not potatoes, but oil. It was not $25,000, but $250,000. And it was not a profit, but a loss. And one more thing about this introduction—it was not me who lost the money; it was my brother."

As the story illustrates, truth matters. And in some situations, it *really* matters.

There was a time not so long ago, in fact, when certain truths were accepted and agreed upon by the majority of people. In our modern era, however, truth has become relative—it can change according to circumstances and differing perspectives. In a study by researcher George Barna of Americans between ages twenty-six and forty-four, only 20 percent of those surveyed strongly disagreed with the statement "There is no such thing as absolute truth; different people can define truth in different ways and still be correct."[1] Shockingly, only 27 percent of those who described themselves as born-again Christians strongly disagreed!

The whole idea that truth is relative contradicts God's Word. As the apostle Paul wrote, "All Scripture is inspired by God and is useful to teach us what is true and to make us realize what is wrong in our lives. It straightens us out and teaches us to do what is right" (2 Timothy 3:16).

## What Is "Truth"?

If you were asked to describe *absolute truth,* what would you say? By what standard can we measure an issue or a statement to determine if it is truth or not? If you don't believe there is such a thing as absolute truth, how do you find *anything* to be true and trustworthy? Let me give you three qualities of absolute truth:

### Absolute Truth Is Internally Consistent

No matter which way you approach a true statement, it remains unassailably true. When we say that our God is absolute truth, we mean that He is internally consistent in His character and being. There is no contradiction within the context and framework of His nature.

Internal consistency of character is vital to all of God's attributes. If you can prove that God is not truthful in any aspect of who He is and how He acts, then His other qualities have no validity. If He were not absolutely consistent, then God's unlimited power, for example, could be compromised by His love. He would be like a powerful president of a country who fails to take action against evil because he lets his emotions, his misguided notions of love, negate his power.

## ABSOLUTE TRUTH IS ALWAYS TRUE

Not everything qualifies as absolute truth. For example, if you said, "Today, the interest rate for home mortgages is at 6.5 percent," that could be true for you living in America. But for someone living in Brazil, the interest rate might be 50 percent. And a month from now, the interest rate for you could change to 8 percent. Because interest rates fluctuate, the percentage rate is not true for all people in all places at all times.

On the other hand, if you say, "Adultery is always wrong," you would be stating an absolute truth. Whether you live in Bangladesh, Japan, or the United States, adultery is still wrong. Adultery was just as wrong a thousand years ago as it is today. Adultery is wrong for the wife living with the alcoholic husband or the business or military person separated from a spouse by extended travel.

## ABSOLUTE TRUTH HAS ITS SOURCE IN OUR HOLY GOD

No human can think up or discover a new truth. Truth has always existed in God's nature; He is the author of truth. Our holy God, who is present everywhere and knows all things, has total understanding of what is real, what is right, and what is true. Whatever He says is completely accurate.

Regarding God's truthfulness, Balaam said, "God is not a man, that he should lie, nor a son of man, that he should change his mind. Does he speak and then not act? Does he promise and not fulfill?" (Numbers 23:19 NIV). Whatever God says is absolutely right. Whatever He promises will always be fulfilled.

We must always measure our beliefs by the truth in God's Word. Since He is the author of truth, He is the only One who can guide us to absolute truth. With Him, we see truth face-to-face. Any other guide will only lead us into confusion and deception.

Have you ever heard the phrase "It's written in stone"? This usually refers to a statement that cannot be changed or revised. The phrase comes from the Old Testament account of when God gave the Ten Commandments. About two months after the Israelites had escaped slavery in Egypt, they reached Mount Sinai, where God revealed Himself to the people. God's holiness and power were clearly evident. Moses went up the mountain into a cloud that looked like a devouring fire and stayed forty days and nights. During that time, God wrote the Ten Commandments with His own finger on tablets of stone. God required His people to obey these timeless, unalterable truths.

Meanwhile, the people, under the leadership of Moses' brother Aaron, began to think that Moses would never return. So Aaron built them a golden calf to take God's place. Aware of the people's disobedience, God told Moses to go back down the mountain. As Moses strode downward clutching the stone tablets, he heard the clamor of celebration. When he got near, he saw God's people worshiping a golden calf. The people who had promised to obey all of God's law had already broken one of the Ten Commandments. In anguish and anger over the sight, Moses hurled the tablets to the ground, shattering them.

Then God said to Moses: "Prepare two stone tablets like the first ones. I will write on them the same words that were on the tablets you smashed" (Exodus 34:1). Once more Moses climbed that cloud-covered mountain; once more God etched the Ten Commandments into stone with His finger.

Do you see the picture of absolute truth in this account? God wrote the commandments in stone. No one can erase or alter them; they are absolute truth. Moses, in his anger, shattered the stone tablets. As humans we can break God's commandments, but we cannot change them. The broken laws are not any less true. After the first tablets were shattered, God just wrote them on stone once more.

## GOD SHOWS US THE TRUTH

Because God knows the end from the beginning, not one of His statements ever turns out to be changeable or variable. God wants us to know the absolute truth, so He has taken the initiative to show us truth in several ways: in His Word, the Bible; by the life, death, and resurrection of His Son; and through His Holy Spirit.

### THE BIBLE

The Bible is God's absolute truth in written form. We can read it, memorize it, and meditate on it. When Jesus was praying for His disciples, He asked God to "sanctify them by the truth; your word is truth" (John 17:17 NIV). God uses the Bible to reveal truth about himself, us, and life. There is no way anyone can live a holy, satisfying, fulfilled life without spending regular time in the Word of God.

### JESUS CHRIST

But truth is not just a concept; it is embodied in a person— Jesus Christ. Jesus proclaimed, "I am the way, the truth, and the life. No one can come to the Father except through me"

(John 14:6). While many people claim to *know* the truth, only Jesus could honestly claim to *be* the truth. Jesus is also the messenger of truth. He said, "I came to bring truth to the world. All who love the truth recognize that what I say is true" (John 18:37).

### THE HOLY SPIRIT

As Christians, we have the Holy Spirit living within us. One of His primary responsibilities is to reveal truth to us. In fact, Jesus called Him "the Spirit of truth." Jesus told His disciples, "I will ask the Father, and he will give you another Counselor to be with you for ever—the Spirit of truth" (John 14:16–17 NIV). The Holy Spirit is Christ's representative who communicates directly with us, illuminates God's truth, and gives us the power to obey that truth. In fact, when we worship God, we are to worship Him in spirit and in truth. Spirit-filled worship leads us to a reverence for God's truth, which in turn leads us to daily obedience. We put our worship into action when we say yes to God's truth in each and every decision of our lives.

> *God's truth frees us to live as He has intended.*

I often use the illustration that the Holy Spirit represents one wing of an airplane and that the Word of God represents the other. Our Lord Jesus Christ is the Pilot. No airplane will fly with just one wing. If we do not rely on the Holy Spirit to guide us and also saturate ourselves with God's truth—His holy, inspired, inerrant truth—then our holy life will not fly. Jesus promised, "If you hold to my teaching, you are really my disciples. Then you will know the truth, and the truth will set you free" (John 8:31–32 NIV). God's truth frees us to live as He has intended. We must also allow Jesus to be the Navigator of our plans, desires, wills, and emotions, for He is the truth.

Do your decisions and lifestyle demonstrate that you are listening to Jesus? Or have you bought into the lies of popular culture? Are you consistently spending time discovering truth in God's Word? Only those who diligently seek it in the right places will find truth.

We do not need to be confused about what is right or wrong—we can look to God's Word. We cannot

*Do your decisions and lifestyle demonstrate that you are listening to Jesus?*

complain that we do not have an example of how to put God's truth into practice—we have the truth in the flesh, Jesus Christ. And we cannot excuse ourselves from knowing and following God's truth—we have the power of the Holy Spirit, who leads us into all truth. Because God is absolute truth, you can believe what He says and live accordingly.

---

1. *Barna Report, 1997: American Witness* (Dallas, Texas: Word Publishing, 1997).

THE LORD IS RIGHTEOUS IN ALL HIS WAYS
AND LOVING TOWARD ALL HE HAS MADE.

PSALM 145:17 NIV

# 11

# God Is Righteous

How can there be so many different views about what is right and what is wrong? Why are moral issues no longer seen as black or white but rather as varying shades of gray? Why do the standards of morality constantly change within our society?

Today, the distinction between right and wrong is becoming increasingly blurred. People passionately defend their sinful actions. What is right has become a matter of interpretation by the individual, the community, or the courts. However, this view is absolutely wrong because it assumes that public opinion and government legislation provide the ultimate criterion for determining what is right. But our sovereign God sets the standards for His creation. His standards do not change; they are timeless. And our American society, like many Western nations, was built on the biblical principles of right and wrong.

## THE "RIGHTNESS" OF MORAL LAWS

Our culture understands how important it is to be "right" about certain things.

When an architect designs a hundred-story skyscraper, he takes immense precautions to have the building's foundation perfectly level. If the footings are off even a fraction of an inch, there will be tremendous consequences. The farther up he builds on an uneven foundation, the more unstable the skyscraper becomes.

Scientists at Mission Control in Houston also know the importance of being "right" when guiding a spaceship back to Earth. If the trajectory of reentry into Earth's atmosphere is off just a little bit, the spaceship will encounter too much friction and burn up before it reaches the ground.

What's more, consider how a speed-skating race is conducted. Two lanes circle the track. While the skaters compete against each other, they are required to stay in their own lane. If one skater crosses the line into the other lane, he is disqualified and loses the race.

Although most people understand the importance of laying the *right* foundation, having the *right* reentry trajectory, or staying in the *right* lane, they have problems understanding the *rightness* of moral laws. When it comes to stealing, for example, most people divide stealing into categories like "borrowing," petty theft, robbery, and embezzlement. They feel that some categories are okay, such as taking a few supplies from their employer or school or keeping the excess when a cashier gives them too much

*God has never had to reverse a decision when He learned more facts.*

change. But to them it would be wrong to break into someone's home or rob a bank. Moral laws, they believe, are not as rigid as other laws. Therefore, we can bend them a little without incurring any penalty.

But that is contrary to how God sees His righteous laws.

It is easy to understand God's righteous role as Creator. Everything He created functions according to the laws applying to its creation. All His natural laws perform the way He intends for the good of His creation. Look at the way a coastal marsh works. Each day, tides bring fresh nutrients for the millions of tiny plants that grow in the soil and water. At high tide, all kinds of shellfish dine on these tiny plants. Fish such as spotted sea trout spawn in the calm water, and the tiny hatchlings feed in their own little marshy nursery. Ducks and other birds build nests to raise their young. A stew of vegetation provides a smorgasbord for the ducklings and goslings. Natural laws and processes work together as a system to benefit all of God's creation.

*God's spiritual laws are every bit as absolute as His physical laws. If we break God's natural laws, we pay the consequences.*

Just as God created nature in its right order, He also created the moral realm to function in its right order. We learned previously that God is holy. But His holiness and His righteousness are not the same. Holiness is a condition of purity or freedom from sin. God's righteousness is the quality or attribute of God that causes Him to act in accordance with His own nature, will, and law. In other words, holiness describes God's nature; righteousness describes how God acts according to His holiness. God's laws are holy because they come from His nature. God's standards for enforcing His laws are always righteous.

## HOW RIGHTEOUS IS GOD?

Everything God does is perfectly right in every way. As David said, "The LORD is righteous in all his ways and loving toward all he has made" (Psalm 145:17 NIV). For God, righteousness is not an external standard that He must adhere to; righteousness is part of His very nature. It is impossible for God to do anything wrong. He has never made a wrong determination. He has never had to reverse a decision when He learned more facts.

*God's spiritual laws are the pillars for justice and morality within any nation.*

God does not struggle with right and wrong. The psalmist declares, "Righteous are you, O LORD, and your laws are right" (Psalm 119:137 NIV). His laws reflect His own righteous nature and the moral perfection of His character. Cultural bias, a lack of knowledge, or any other factor does not alter His rulings.

God's spiritual laws are every bit as absolute as His physical laws. If we break God's natural laws, we pay the consequences. For example, if you jump from the Empire State Building in New York City, the law of gravity will guarantee your death. Likewise, if you lock yourself in a garage and breathe carbon monoxide instead of the oxygen your body needs, you will die.

God's spiritual laws are no less binding. As the perfect Judge and Lawgiver, God is also the Law Enforcer. His laws lay out the responsibilities for which God holds us accountable. They serve as a yardstick by which God measures our righteousness. When His laws are broken, He must punish anyone who defies His righteous laws.

You may wonder why God is so exacting about His spiritual laws. He did not make rules just for the "fun of it." His righteous laws focus on standards for acting rightly toward one another. Consequently, God's spiritual laws are the pillars for justice and morality within any nation. When national leaders reject and disobey God, they cut their nation loose from the anchor of morality. Without God, they lose their moral compass and doom their society to injustice, dishonesty, and depravity.

Ever since Adam and Eve first disobeyed God, every person has been born with a sinful nature that insists on exerting self-will. And because of our sinful nature, it is impossible for us to live the righteous life God demands. We are so fortunate that "the LORD is gracious and righteous; our God is full of compassion" (Psalm 116:5 NIV). Otherwise we would be doomed by our lack of righteousness. Our righteousness

*His laws lay out the responsibilities for which God holds us accountable. They serve as a yardstick by which God measures our righteousness.*

does not depend on what we do, but in whom we place our faith. As the apostle Paul explained:

> We are made right in God's sight when we trust in Jesus
> Christ to take away our sins. And we all can be saved in
> this same way, no matter who we are or what we have
> done.

For all have sinned; all fall short of God's glorious standard.
Yet now God in his gracious kindness declares us not guilty.
He has done this through Christ Jesus, who has freed us by
taking away our sins. For God sent Jesus to take the punishment for our sins and to satisfy God's anger against us.
We are made right with God when we believe that Jesus
shed his blood, sacrificing his life for us.

ROMANS 3:22–25

There was not anything we could do to earn this gift of
grace. We accepted it by faith. Now God no longer sees our
sinfulness, but only the right-
eousness of Christ that covers
us. When we put our faith in
Christ, we received a new
nature—one of holiness and
righteousness. Christ wants us to
display His righteousness in our new life. We are commanded:
"Throw off your old evil nature and your former way of life,
which is rotten through and through, full of lust and deception.
Instead, there must be a spiritual renewal of your thoughts and
attitudes. You must display a new nature because you are a new
person, created in God's likeness—righteous, holy, and true"
(Ephesians 4:22–24).

> *The secret to changing bad habits is to turn the problem over to God.*

Yet we sometimes attempt to achieve righteousness under
our own power. That never works. We cannot live righteously
without the enabling of the Holy Spirit, and His power is
released through our faith. For example, if a person has a
problem with swearing, he could try his hardest to quit using
foul language. For the most part, he would be able to control
his tongue, but when someone cuts him off on the freeway or

breaks in front of him in a line, his mouth spews curse words before he even realizes what he is saying. All his efforts to control this reaction come to nothing.

The secret to changing bad habits is to turn the problem over to God. By faith, admit that you are helpless to change your bad habit. As you walk in the Spirit moment by moment, your heart is prepared to act righteously the next time you are tempted to do wrong. Trust God to take over and work out the problem. This will make the difference in your reaction and the results of the problem.

We have discussed confessing sin when our lives take a turn from God's perfect standard, but God wants us to do more than that. Henry Blackaby and Claude King explain in their book *Experiencing God*, "God wants you to have no hindrances to a love relationship with Him in your life. Once God has spoken to you through His Word, how you respond is crucial. You must adjust your life to the truth."[1]

This means adjusting your life in areas where you have been disobeying Him. Adjusting your standards also may mean making changes in your life that comply with God's leading. Knowing God's truth and holiness always leads to righteous action. Because God is righteous, you can live by His standards.

---

1. Henry T. Blackaby and Claude V. King, *Experiencing God* (Nashville, Tenn.: Broadman & Holman, 1994), p. 167.

———————❖———————

"Everything he does is just and fair.
He is a faithful God who does no wrong;
how just and upright he is!"

Deuteronomy 32:4

———————————

# 12

# God Is Just

D o you ever wonder what happened to justice? Why is it becoming increasingly elusive? What has gone wrong with the man-made judicial system?

Justice is a pillar of any society. It vindicates the innocent and punishes the guilty. All too often, though, this standard is compromised for personal gain. Today, people are becoming less concerned about doing what is right. Instead, they look for ways to cover their tracks, believing they will never get caught. If their transgression is discovered, they assume they will never be convicted. If they are found guilty, they can always appeal. If the appeal is denied, they will likely serve only a fraction of their sentence anyway.

Since our justice system can often be manipulated, many people mistakenly believe they can manipulate God's system of justice as well. They think that their excuses and alibis fool God. But how wrong they are! God told Jeremiah, "I the LORD search the heart and examine the mind, to reward a man according to his conduct, according to what his deeds deserve"

(17:10 NIV). God will always act according to what is morally upright or good.

## GOD'S JUSTICE

Justice is not an external system to which God tries to adhere. He did not have to go to law school to learn how to apply the law. His justice comes out of His inner being and is based on His holiness, truthfulness, and righteousness. Moses observed, "Everything he does is just and fair. He is a faithful God who does no wrong; how just and upright he is!" (Deuteronomy 32:4).

God cannot be bribed or corrupted, because His judgments are grounded in integrity. He has all the facts at His disposal, so He cannot be fooled. His decisions are always based upon absolute truth. And when God pronounces judgment, He has the power to carry out the punishment.

God's standard is the benchmark by which all human behavior is measured. God "always acts in a way consistent with the requirements of His character as revealed in His law. He rules His creation with honesty. He keeps His word. He renders to all His creatures their due."[1]

God's attributes assure us of justice. If He were not all-knowing, how could He know whether we sinned willingly or manipulated the facts to serve our purposes? If He were not present everywhere at once, how could He know all the circumstances surrounding the issue before Him? If He were not all-wise, how could He carry out the judgment in a totally fair way?

Since God is omnipotent, whatever He decides to do, He can carry out. He does not have to ask anyone's permission; He does not need a police force to back Him up. In His courtroom, His authority is the last word. No one can appeal His decisions. That is why He is pictured in heaven on a throne. As Ruler of the universe, His authority is total and complete.

God also follows laws—which He established. We find them in His Word as commands and rules. There is no higher law than God's laws. Not only is He the Judge,

> *A reverential fear of God will help us avoid doing anything to hinder our relationship with Him.*

but He is also the Lawmaker. Since God's laws are perfect, His justice is also without flaw. As the holy and righteous sovereign of the universe, God cannot ignore or overlook any act of sin. God hates sin with a holy passion. David wrote, "God is a judge who is perfectly fair. He is angry with the wicked every day" (Psalm 7:11).

God's anger over sin should never be underestimated: "You spread out our sins before you—our secret sins—and you see them all. We live our lives beneath your wrath.... Who can comprehend the power of your anger? Your wrath is as awesome as the fear you deserve" (Psalm 90:8–11).

## STAYING IN FELLOWSHIP WITH GOD

I urge you to live in reverential fear of God, continually searching His Word and examining your heart for sins that you need to confess to Him. One of the greatest truths I have discovered in over fifty years of walking with the Lord is a concept I call "Spiritual Breathing." This process is similar to physical breathing. As we become aware of our sins, we "exhale" by confessing our sin. Then we "inhale" to appropriate the power of the Holy Spirit, based on God's command to be filled with the Spirit. We can know that God will fill, enable, and equip us, because He promised to hear and answer our prayers in accordance with His perfect will.

This spiritual principle has allowed me to walk in fellowship with God and help others come to know and serve Him. This is the privilege of every believer.

## GETTING AWAY WITH WRONGDOING?

The Bible tells us, "God will bring every deed into judgment, including every hidden thing, whether it is good or evil" (Ecclesiastes 12:14 NIV). Yet I suppose there have been times when you have asked, "Why are the wicked so prosperous? Why are evil people so happy?" (Jeremiah 12:1).

There may be several reasons why someone appears to be getting away with wrongdoing and avoiding punishment.

> *God delays His judgment because He patiently provides an opportunity for repentance.*

God delays His judgment because He patiently provides an opportunity for repentance. But while God is waiting for repentance, the severity of future punishment is mounting.

Sometimes we do not recognize God's judgment because it occurs in a way that we did not expect. As Paul explained, "Do not be deceived: God cannot be mocked. A man reaps what he sows" (Galatians 6:7 NIV). The more seeds of sin a person sows, the more harm will be caused. Sin is like an addictive poison. If you drink just a little bit of poison, you may only get sick. But if you keep on drinking poison, it will eventually kill you.

We cannot thumb our noses at God's righteous principles and not expect to experience the just consequences of our actions. A reverential fear of God will help us avoid doing anything to hinder our relationship with Him.

God predicts judgment for the ungodly: "It is mine to avenge; I will repay. In due time their foot will slip; their day of disaster is near and their doom rushes upon them" (Deuteronomy 32:35 NIV). Yet many live as though they will never be judged. They scoff at the idea of an eternal hell. The final judgment has, however, been part of the biblical message for thousands of years. The Holy Spirit inspired Paul to write this ominous warning:

> Because of your stubbornness and your unrepentant heart, you are storing up wrath against yourself for the day of God's wrath, when his righteous judgment will be revealed. God "will give to each person according to what he has done." To those who by persistence in doing good seek glory, honor and immortality, he will give eternal life. But for those who are self-seeking and who reject the truth and follow evil, there will be wrath and anger.
>
> ROMANS 2:5–8 NIV

Those are hard words from a holy, just God. In Revelation, we have a visual description of that final Judgment Day of wrath:

> Then I saw a great white throne and him who was seated on it. Earth and sky fled from his presence, and there was no place for them. And I saw the dead, great and small, standing before the throne, and books were opened. Another book was opened, which is the book of life. The dead were judged according to what they had done as recorded in the books. The sea gave up the dead that were in it, and death and Hades gave up the dead that were in them, and each person was judged according to what he

had done. Then death and Hades were thrown into the lake of fire. The lake of fire is the second death. If anyone's name was not found written in the book of life, he was thrown into the lake of fire.

REVELATION 20:11–15 NIV

I never want to face that judgment seat! We can be thankful that those of us who have trusted Christ will not appear before the Great White Throne judgment of sinners. But all believers will appear before the Judgment Seat of Christ. Christ will evaluate each believer's life to determine rewards for faithful obedience and service or loss for disobedience. As Paul said, "We must all stand before Christ to be judged. We will each receive whatever we deserve for the good or evil we have done in our bodies" (2 Corinthians 5:10).

> *Are you living for the glory of God or for self-satisfaction? There is an incredible reward awaiting the person who seeks to glorify God.*

Our just God is not primarily concerned with punishing disobedience, but with rewarding right behavior. Yet God will reward only those who accept Christ's penalty for sin, because His payment for our sins opened the way for God to reward us for what we do for Him.

Are you living for the glory of God or for self-satisfaction? There is an incredible reward awaiting the person who seeks to glorify God. Paul was so sure of this reward that he said, "Whatever you do, work at it with all your heart, as working for the Lord, not for men, since you know that you will receive an inheritance from the Lord as a reward. It is the Lord Christ you are serving" (Colossians 3:23–24 NIV).

Do you trust God's perfect justice? It is undergirded by His holiness, truth, and righteousness and is perfectly administered through His omniscience, omnipotence, and omnipresence. He is the perfect Judge. Although your salvation is secured by faith in Jesus Christ, your good works confirm that you are a child of God and determine the rewards you will receive from Him. Because God is just, He will always treat you fairly.

---

1. *Wycliffe Bible Encyclopedia* (Chicago: Moody Press, 1975) vol. 1, p. 981.

FOR THE LORD IS GOOD. HIS UNFAILING
LOVE CONTINUES FOREVER.

PSALM 100:5

# 13

# God Is Love and Mercy

Love is a universal need of all humanity. Everyone wants to be loved. But our world understands very little about true love. We must turn to God to understand what love is all about.

In New Testament times, there were three primary words for love: *eros* (sensual love), *phileo* (brotherly love), and *agape* (unconditional, supernatural love). Our world speaks mainly of *eros* or *phileo* love, but God's love is *agape*—the purest, deepest kind of love.

God is the source of all love. The quality is the supreme expression of God's personhood and flows out of His goodness. It affects all His other attributes. The Bible does not say, "God is holiness" or "God is power," but "God is love" (1 John 4:8). While people are sometimes willing to violate standards of honesty, righteousness, and morality in order to please others, God never compromises His integrity. His love does not suppress or negate any of His other attributes.

## GOD'S SUPERNATURAL LOVE

God's love is unconditional. It is not based on how good you are or what you do to bring Him pleasure. He loves you because He is God and you are His creation. The psalmist proclaimed, "For the LORD is good. His unfailing love continues forever" (100:5). God's love will not be terminated because of disappointment or a change of heart. God's heart overflows with His supernatural and unconditional love for us.

Many years ago, I spoke on God's unconditional love at a missions conference for the famous Park Street Church in Boston. A missionary with whom I had attended seminary twenty years earlier approached me afterward.

"I would never preach a sermon like that," he scolded. "I leave talking about God's love to the theological liberals. My message emphasizes *faith*."

This man had lost sight of one of God's greatest qualities. God's love is the only reason we exist. It is the *why* of creation, whereas His power is the *how*. Love flows from Him as a pure river of grace and mercy without detracting in any way from His holiness and righteousness. Everywhere we look, we see evidence of God's loving concern for our well-being.

God's love is expressed to all people, not just those who love Him. He loved us first before we loved Him—even when we were unlovable. That is hard for us to accept at times. Why would God stoop to love such unworthy people as we are? Our mortal minds cannot comprehend its vastness or its consistency. We will never be able to know *why*, but we can believe it is true, causing us to love, appreciate, worship, and praise Him all the more in return.

God's love is a gift to all who will receive it by faith; He offers it to us freely. Nothing we do will make God love us any more; nothing we do will make Him love us any less. He loves us because He is gracious—not because of who we are, but because of who He is.

Usually, in our world, the rich, beautiful, talented, and intelligent receive the most attention and "love." But our social situation has no bearing on God's love for us. When Jesus entered Jericho, He had to pass by that greedy tax collector Zacchaeus, who was shunned by everyone in town. Zacchaeus' spiritual hunger was so great that he climbed up a tree to see Jesus. When Jesus passed by, He looked up and said, "Zacchaeus, come down immediately. I must stay at your house today" (Luke 19:5 NIV). Zacchaeus did not need a second invitation. Scrambling out of the tree, he quickly welcomed Jesus into his home.

God's love reaches out to the most socially despised and brings them within the circle of His love. God's love frees a person from sin and despair—no matter who that person is.

God's sacrifice in planning for our salvation was set in motion in eternity past: "He chose us in him before the creation of the world to be holy and blameless in his sight.

*God's love will not be terminated because of disappointment or a change of heart.*

In love he predestined us to be adopted as his sons through Jesus Christ" (Ephesians 1:4–5 NIV). There was never a moment when God did not intend to make the ultimate sacrifice for us. He planned to leave heaven's glory, beauty, and peace and take on the body of a man.

When we receive Jesus as our Savior and Lord, God

envelops and infuses us with His everlasting love. We enter into a special eternal relationship with Him. John recognized this and exclaimed: "How great is the love the Father has lavished on us, that we should be called children of God!" (1 John 3:1 NIV). This love will be with us for eternity.

Nothing we do will take away His love for us. Paul said, "I am convinced that nothing can ever separate us from his love. Death can't, and life can't. The angels can't, and the demons can't. Our fears for today, our worries about tomorrow, and even the powers of hell can't keep God's love away. Whether we are high above the sky or in the deepest ocean, nothing in all creation will ever be able to separate us from the love of God that is revealed in Christ Jesus our Lord" (Romans 8:38–39). We need never fear that His blessings are a disguise for other intentions.

The apostle John said, "This is love: not that we loved God, but that he loved us and sent his Son as an atoning sacrifice for our sins" (1 John 4:10 NIV). Jesus gave His life on your behalf. He could not have sacrificed any more. We, in turn, are to love God wholeheartedly. Jesus declared: "'Love the Lord your God with all your heart and with all your soul and with all your mind.' This is the first and greatest commandment" (Matthew 22:37–38 NIV). God, in His sovereignty, has created us so we find our greatest joy and fulfillment in loving Him.

God enables us to be channels of His supernatural love. On our own, we are incapable of loving as we should, but God has for us an unending supply of His divine love. It is for us to claim, to enjoy, and to share with others. When believers begin to love God, love their neighbors as themselves, and love their enemies, society will change for the better. Then the world today, as in the first century, will marvel when it sees and experiences the transforming power of God's love.

We worship our loving God not as a religious exercise or ritual, but with a sincere response to the love He has already shown for us! Every day, praise Him for His unconditional, perfect love. Praise Him when you wake up in the morning, thank Him as you work, and tell Him how much you love Him before you go to sleep. Respond to His limitless, ever-present love to you by expressing your heart of love to Him. Because God is love, He is unconditionally committed to your well-being.

## GOD IS MERCIFUL

The wretched, shackled prisoner trembled with fear as he stood before the imposing bench of the toughest, fairest judge in the district. "You have been found guilty," the judge solemnly announced. Courtroom observers held their breath, waiting for the most severe punishment possible.

Without a doubt, the man was guilty. The evidence was clear. The judge had no choice but to pronounce a death sentence. There were no appeals for the horrendous crime, no stays of execution allowed.

Suddenly, to everyone's shock, the judge did something unprecedented in legal history. He said to the prisoner, "Justice must be served. You are guilty. You are totally unlovable. Nevertheless, I love you, in spite of yourself. And because of my love for you, I have decided to take your place. I will bear your punishment for you. I will die in your place. You are a free man. You can go now." The judge's gavel pounded. The courtroom was silent.

After a stunned moment, courtroom guards unlocked the prisoner's handcuffs and leg irons, removed the judge's robe, and snapped the irons on his wrists and ankles. As the judge was led away to death row, the shocked prisoner numbly walked through the courtroom door to freedom, tears of gratitude streaming down his cheeks.

This, of course, is an allegory about God's mercy. God is the judge. Since He is perfectly just, all His actions must serve the universal law of justice. We are like the prisoner. We all deserve the death sentence because we are all guilty of numerous sins: "All have sinned and fall short of the glory of God" (Romans 3:23 NIV). In His fairness, God must judge our sin with the harshest punishment. He cannot allow us to inhabit His perfect heaven, that place without a spot of uncleanness, a thought of wrongdoing, or a charge of guilt.

## GOD'S MERCY THROUGH JESUS CHRIST

In the supreme act of mercy, God displayed divine favor and forbearance to us guilty offenders. As James wrote, "[The Lord] is full of tenderness and mercy" (5:11). He took our punishment upon Himself. That is what Jesus Christ did for us at Calvary: "The gift of God is eternal life in Christ Jesus our Lord" (Romans 6:23 NIV). By His sacrifice, all who put their trust in Him are declared "not guilty."

God's very nature desires to relieve you of the self-imposed misery and distress you experience because of your sin. The fact is that when we sin, we will never be excused from the penalty. If that sounds cruel and unfair, here is the good news: Jesus provided a dramatic reprieve from our sentence and punishment. As Peter explained, "[Jesus] personally carried away our sins in his own body on the cross so we can be dead to sin and live for what is right. You have been healed by his wounds!" (1 Peter 2:24). When Jesus came, His blood was spilled so we could experience God's mercy. Jesus' sacrifice is the ultimate expression of God's mercy.

Jesus Christ's sacrifice on the cross satisfied God's just nature. God, the divine Judge, showed mercy and clemency for us guilty sinners. It is the mercy of God that sees man weighed down by sin and therefore in a sorry and pitiful condition, needing divine help. At the cross, God's attributes of *both* justice and mercy found complete fulfillment.

## QUALITIES OF GOD'S MERCY

God's mercy does not end with the forgiveness of our sins. He provides us an abundant life that is much more than we deserve or could ever expect. In His mercy, He provides what we need to begin growing in His Spirit. He shows us compassion as we walk with Him day by day. And His mercy also means that He will discipline us as a loving father disciplines his child. He has a plan for our lives that will bring us to maturity in His grace.

God's mercy enables us to break free from the habits of sin that have bound us. As a result, we can have peace, joy, fulfillment, and purpose. We will find the true meaning for living—serving God. We will find the true joy in life—serving others. We will find true peace and fulfillment—living in God's presence and will, moment by moment.

What astounds me is that God genuinely feels pity and compassion for us during our trials and difficulties. We have the assurance that "the LORD comforts his people and will have compassion on his afflicted ones" (Isaiah 49:13 NIV). Our loving Father does not just feel our pain; He wants to relieve our pain. He will if we trust and obey Him.

The Gospels are filled with examples of how Jesus was moved with compassion to help those who were sick, suffering, and needy. The woman who had been ill with bleeding for many years was healed when she touched His garment. Jesus reached out His hands and healed the blind man, Bartimaeus, and the ten lepers. And the woman caught in adultery? Jesus spoke compassionately to her and forgave her: "Neither do I [condemn you]. Go and sin no more" (John 8:11). We can be sure that our merciful God is beside us through every trial we face and every pain we endure.

If you are a parent, you know that your feelings of compassion and mercy toward your child will often be tested. At times you will have to exercise discipline. A child does not know he is loved unless his parents set up behavior boundaries and then enforce them in love and fairness.

*His mercy toward the unrepentant sinner does not last forever.*

The loved child understands when someone cares enough to take the time to correct wrong behavior. That is the way God is with us. When we become part of His family through our spiritual birth, He corrects and rebukes us for the things we do wrong. As we listen to His Spirit and obey His Word, we become fulfilled, joyful members of His family.

God wants you to be merciful to others in gratitude for the mercy He has extended to you. In the Sermon on the Mount, Jesus declared, "God blesses those who are merciful, for they will be shown mercy" (Matthew 5:7). In fact, Jesus said, "If you refuse to forgive others, your Father will not forgive your sins" (Matthew 6:15). God's mercy flows to those who show mercy to others.

Although God's mercy toward His own people extends throughout eternity, His mercy toward the unrepentant sinner does not last forever.

Before Alexander the Great would lay siege to a city, he would set up a light, giving notice to those who lived within the city that if they came to him while that light was still burning, he would spare their lives. But once the light was out, no mercy was to be expected. In much the same way, God sets up light after light and waits year after year for sinners to come to Him so they may have eternal life. He does not want anyone to perish, so He is giving more time for everyone to repent. But a time is coming when there will be no more mercy. Those who feel they can wait until later to receive God's offer of mercy can never be sure that they will have the time or opportunity to receive His forgiveness.

> *Because God is merciful, He forgives all your sins when you sincerely confess them.*

In light of His mercy to us, our hearts should be filled with gratitude, praise, and worship. Author David Morris writes, "When Jesus came to earth, He changed seats with us and took on all our sin, rejection, and shame so we could see ourselves from His perspective."[1] We should never lose the awe and appreciation of what God has done for us. We once wore filthy garments stained by sin and corruption; now we are clothed in spotless robes of righteousness.

Because of God's great compassion, He generously bestows on you His grace, mercy, and peace. He demonstrates His grace by showering you with blessings you do not deserve.

He displays His great mercy by withholding the punishment you so rightfully deserve. And God's many expressions of grace and mercy will produce in you—peace! Because God is merciful, He forgives all your sins when you sincerely confess them.

---

1. David Morris, *A Lifestyle of Worship* (Ventura, Calif.: Renew Books, 1998), p. 201.

# 14

# God Is Faithful

All of us understand to some degree how an automobile engine functions. Pistons, fan belts, water pumps, and thousands of moving parts all whirl around within a small space, generating power for us to drive our car. Each part in the motor has a different role to play in helping the engine function as it should. If one piece gets even a fraction of an inch out of line, the engine malfunctions. At the same time, oil and coolant circulate to keep the machinery running smoothly. The parts all work together harmoniously to enable the whole engine to do its job.

That is the way God's attributes function, too. If you took away love, God's character would not be complete. God's love works with all other attributes, like His justice, to produce the right kind of results. We can compare God's faithfulness to the oil in the engine that keeps the internal parts running smoothly. God's faithfulness means that each attribute in His character is working at full capacity at all times.

God's faithfulness is at the core of God's nature. The psalmist wrote, "O LORD God Almighty! Where is there anyone as mighty as you, LORD? Faithfulness is your very character" (89:8). God is all-knowing, all-powerful, ever-present, holy, righteous, merciful, and loving because He is faithful to His own character. He never changes any of His attributes to accommodate someone else's wishes. Paul drew on that knowledge when he wrote to the Thessalonians that they could depend on God because "the one who calls you is faithful and he will do it" (1 Thessalonians 5:24 NIV).

> *In His faithfulness, God keeps His covenants or promises—without fail.*

In His faithfulness, God keeps His covenants or promises—without fail. The writer of Hebrews declared, "Without wavering, let us hold tightly to the hope we say we have, for God can be trusted to keep his promise" (10:23). God is ready and able to deliver on all He has promised. Paul wrote, "No matter how many promises God has made, they are 'Yes' in Christ. And so through him the 'Amen' [so be it] is spoken by us to the glory of God" (2 Corinthians 1:20 NIV).

Although God has promised us all the strength and help we will ever need, many of us try to "go it alone." We seem unaware of the boundless resources God has provided in the person of the Holy Spirit and His faithfulness to bring about everything He promised to do. As a result, we become unfulfilled, fruitless, and spiritually malnourished. Frantically hurrying about in our self-imposed spiritual poverty, we never "cash the checks" of joy, peace, and abundance that are in our hands. No wonder we think at times that God has abandoned us.

God is faithful to help you in adversity. We all experience hard times in our lives. These struggles with sickness, danger, financial problems, grief, or depression happen to each of us at times. But these only prompt us to cling ever tighter to God—not to turn away from Him, blaming Him for causing or allowing all our troubles. He does not promise to prevent problems from coming into our lives, but He does promise to go through them with us. We can rely on God to use these situations to build character and faith in our lives.

God does not promise to make life easy for us. But He promises to protect us from anything that is not in the center of His will. He will be there by our side as we walk through all the difficulties and trials that come our way.

## GREAT IS HIS FAITHFULNESS

God is faithful to protect you from temptation and the Evil One. The apostle Paul wrote to the church in Corinth, "God is faithful. He will keep the temptation from becoming so strong that you can't stand up against it. When you are tempted, he will show you a way out so that you will not give in to it" (1 Corinthians 10:13). When you are tempted to sin, focus on God's faithfulness and promise to deliver you from that situation.

Whenever we give in to sin, it is not because we cannot say no. Rather, it is because our focus is on the attractiveness of the temptation, instead of on God's ability to deliver us from that situation. Scripture declares, "The Lord is faithful; he will make you strong and guard you from the evil one" (2 Thessalonians 3:3). If we trust and obey God, He always gives us a way out of any predicament without having to yield to sin.

God is faithful to forgive you even when you are unfaithful. The Holy Spirit inspired John to write, "If we confess our sins to him, he is faithful and just to forgive us and to cleanse us from every wrong" (1 John 1:9). Since John was writing to believers, we have assurance that God has also forgiven all the sins we commit after our spiritual birth as well as those committed before we received Christ as our Savior. No matter when we are unfaithful to God, He will be faithful to forgive when we ask.

God's faithfulness continues beyond the act of giving us new life in Christ and help in times of need. As Paul told the Corinthians:

> Therefore you do not lack any spiritual gift as you eagerly wait for our Lord Jesus Christ to be revealed. He will keep you strong to the end, so that you will be blameless on the day of our Lord Jesus Christ. God, who has called you into fellowship with his Son Jesus Christ our Lord, is faithful.

> 1 CORINTHIANS 1:7–9 NIV

Our faithful God called us into fellowship with His Son—and He committed Himself to our future. That starts with giving us everything we need for our life of worship and witness, for we "do not lack any spiritual gift." Our faithful God never gives us an assignment for which He has not prepared us and enabled us.

God is faithful to purify us from unrighteousness. It is God's plan for us to become holy and advance His kingdom. Paul reminds us in 1 Corinthians 1:8 that He "will keep you strong to the end, so that you will be blameless on the day of our Lord Jesus Christ" (NIV). That is the glorious promise of God to all who follow Him. He will keep us faithful to the end, so that we will be with Him in eternity.

In what area of your life is fear of failure beginning to plague you? Which of your relationships is in danger? What task do you face that you feel you cannot complete? You can make it through anything—for our faithful God is there for you even when you do not feel like a hero of the faith. He is working in your life right now, even though you may not see Him at work or feel His presence. Let His faithfulness in the past fuel your faith and the power of His Holy Spirit fill your soul. Because God is faithful, you can trust Him to always keep His promises.

## GOD NEVER CHANGES

We live in a time of hyper-change. Fashions and trends change weekly; people relocate frequently; technological advances quickly make past achievements obsolete. A way of life that was once familiar and comfortable to us rapidly fades away. This change produces a great deal of stress. As we search for stability, we wonder if there is any permanence to be found. Is there some anchor that will hold us so we will not be swept away by the waves of change washing over society?

There are several reasons we are drawn into the undercurrents of change. For one, sin and our fallen nature promote a process of decay and deterioration. Things get progressively worse when left to themselves. You can understand this if you have ever had to maintain an old house. The water heater needs replacing; the screen door comes off its hinges; the roof leaks.

Another reason we change is because we experience pressure from others or from our circumstances. We alter well-laid plans because of illness or because a family member is in crisis and needs help. An airline goes on strike, so our flight is canceled. All kinds of events make us modify what we want to do.

A third reason we change is because of boredom. We do not want every day to be exactly the same as the last. A little spice and variety make life more enjoyable.

Also, technological achievements and other kinds of improvements stimulate change. For example, computers have dramatically altered the way we do things. No longer do we need to mail a package of important papers; now we can e-mail a file.

> *The influences that cause change in your life have no effect on God.*

Although we live in the midst of constant change, our God never changes. In fact, it is impossible for God to change. The influences that cause change in your life have no effect on God. He will never be stronger or weaker. His knowledge and wisdom will not increase or diminish.

### GOD'S UNCHANGING NATURE

God's unchanging nature applies to all of His attributes as well. We are exceedingly glad that His love, grace, and mercy are unchanging. We appreciate the fact that His holiness cannot change. Emotions or circumstances do not affect God. He "does not change like shifting shadows" (James 1:17 NIV).

One fascinating fact about many of the religions of the world is the unpredictable character of their gods. New Agers believe that everything is God and that God is everything. The source of authority or "truth," they say, is what you experience. In other words, you may believe one thing to be true today, but then an experience tomorrow will change that truth. And what *you* believe to be true will not be true for *me*.

Buddhists believe that salvation is in karma. Kenneth

Latourette, a leading church historian, explains this Buddhist belief: "Karma may be described as the sum of an individual's thoughts and actions in all his previous incarnations. In each incarnation, he modifies his karma for either good or bad.... The ultimate aim is not only to improve one's karma, but to do more, namely, to escape from the endless series of changes, the appalling eternal succession of births and rebirths. This would be salvation."[1]

How different this is from God's simple, unchanging plan of salvation! With God's plan, we know where we stand, what we must do, and the result—an eternal, unalterable place in the family of God.

Animists and idol worshipers have developed their understanding of how their gods work from accumulated folklore. Their gods are so capricious that they must constantly be appeased with sacrifices and a variety of rituals so they will not change the rules of the game. But we can read God's rules in His never-changing Word.

The God of the Bible is unchanging and reliable. He has never altered one bit of His character or His purpose. Theologians call this consistency and dependability God's *immutability*. God has never had to grow or change or develop. God has never had to learn anything—He has always known everything there is to know. God has never had to develop talents or skills—He has always been able to do everything. He has never needed to mature—He has always been perfect in all of His attributes.

God is also not moody, like we are. When I pray to God in the morning, His response will not be different from when I pray to Him at bedtime. When I confront a difficult situation, I have calmness of heart because I know His unchanging Holy

Spirit is present to guide me. Because God's attributes always exist in fullness and in cooperation with each other, God's purposes, motives, thoughts, and actions are forever the same.

The fact that we can depend on God's immutability is tremendously reassuring for us today. We must admit that at times we violate God's unchanging commandments. But we know that when we repent, His unchanging grace brings us forgiveness and favor. We can proclaim God's message of love and forgiveness without fear that He will change the rules the next day.

Isaiah 40:6–8 records that "people are like the grass that dies away. Their beauty fades as quickly as the beauty of flowers in a field. The grass withers, and the flowers fade beneath the breath of the LORD. And so it is with people. The grass withers, and the flowers fade, but the word of our God stands forever."

God does not change what He says based on opinion polls or focus groups. His words and commands are timeless. They are valid throughout all eternity. They apply to every culture, race, and nationality. That is why the Bible has remained relevant throughout the ages and to all civilizations. What God says is always pertinent. It never becomes obsolete. His timeless truth is the surest foundation for anything we attempt.

What's more, God's unchanging purpose gives us eternal significance. Psalm 33:11 states, "The LORD's plans stand firm forever; his intentions can never be shaken." God's plan existed at the beginning of creation and remains the same today. It unfolds in phases and stages, which may give us the impression of change, but His original design has always been consistent.

A story is told of a shipwrecked sailor who clung perilously to a rock until the tide went down. Later, a friend asked him,

"Didn't you shake with fear when you were hanging on the rock?"

He simply replied, "Yes, but the rock didn't."

Life and its uncertainties may shake us, but God—who is the Rock of Ages—does not move. If we cling to Him, His strength sustains us.

Recently, I stood at the gravesites of two dear friends, and as I reflected on their lives, I realized that the most important moment we can experience is our death. When we breathe our last earthly air and take our first breath of the celestial, we transition into the presence of God! This life on earth is but a prelude to eternity. My friends had no fear of crossing over, for they knew the reality of God's unwavering faithfulness to them.

> *This life on earth is but a prelude to eternity.*

We who have placed our trust in the death and resurrection of Jesus Christ have received eternal life. God is committed to our redemption, our Christian walk, and our eternal destiny. God's unchanging nature assures us that we will indeed live with Him forever as He promised. God's commitment is as strong as He is constant.

If you have trusted in Jesus Christ as your Lord and Savior, you can be assured of eternal life. God is committed to your redemption, your spiritual growth, and your eternal destiny. God's commitment to you is as strong as He is eternally constant. He is your Anchor. You can count on God because He never changes.

---

1. Kenneth S. Latourette, *Introducing Buddhism* (New York: Friendship Press, 1956). As quoted in: Russell P. Spittler, *Cults and Isms* (Grand Rapids, Mich.: Baker Book House, 1962), p. 96.

WE CAN COUNT ON GOD,
COMPLETELY AND ABSOLUTELY!

# 15

# Live It!

Are you in the midst of difficult circumstances? Are you facing challenges that seem beyond your ability to cope? Do not despair, because God is with you and He wants to help you.

Allow the truth about Him and His marvelous character to transform your situation and your life. Only then will you experience God's best and become all He wants you to be; only then will you be able to enjoy the life you were created to live.

## GOD IS BIGGER THAN OUR PROBLEMS

There is nothing more important to victorious living than what we believe to be true about God. We must keep our eyes focused on God and His magnificent qualities—instead of becoming preoccupied with our circumstances. God is bigger than any painful situations or vexing problems.

I recently boarded a plane in Europe bound for the United States. A man I had never seen before, whose name I did not even know, boarded the same plane, entered the captain's cabin, and seated himself at the controls. A short time later, the aircraft began to move and soon—by means I do not fully understand—it left the ground. Hours later, we touched down in Orlando.

Not once during our flight did it occur to me to question the man at the controls. I never even thought to ask for his pilot's license or some other identification to prove he was capable of flying that plane. I never asked him to explain to me the physical laws by which he could keep such a heavy object in the air. I have flown millions of miles to most parts of the world. On each of those flights, I have placed my faith in such a stranger, believing he was capable of taking me safely to my destination.

Every day in hundreds of similar situations, believers and nonbelievers alike exercise faith without even thinking twice. If we have such unquestioning faith in fellow human beings—who are not only fallible, but also deliberately sinful at times—how much more should we put all our faith in God? After all, His character and capacity for faithfulness are beyond question.

*Each time He proves Himself faithful in your life, your trust will become stronger.*

God is reliable. He is trustworthy. He cannot be otherwise. His faithfulness ensures that every attribute we have studied so far is available to us. He wants us to reflect His faithfulness on earth. He is the example; we are His ambassadors to the world. Yet even though we understand this fact, in our humanity we must grow in our Christian experience. That means exercising our faith in Him daily to build our trust in God as the faithful One. Each time He proves Himself faithful in our life, our trust will become stronger.

What can you trust God for today that you were unable to trust Him for yesterday? What circumstances do you struggle with that you can begin turning over to Him? Exercising faith is just like exercising a muscle. The more you use it, the stronger it becomes. If you have difficulty trusting God, take baby steps of faith. Then lengthen these steps in the days to come.

Do you remember the story in the Gospels in which Peter walked on water? As long as Peter's gaze was fixed on Jesus, he stayed afloat. But when he looked at the churning waves beneath his feet, he began to sink.

*What can you trust God for today that you were unable to trust Him for yesterday?*

The storms of life are constantly changing, but God remains the same. Do not allow negative circumstances to distract you from remembering God's wonderful attributes and His unchanging commitment to you. He is your Rock. Believe it! Whatever your problems, whatever your circumstances, keep your eyes on Jesus.

Remember that whatever we may go through here on this earth is nothing compared with the eternal life that awaits us with our Lord. God has promised us a future that is indescribably wonderful—a future that is well worth any hardships we may endure during this brief earthly life.

Finally, remember that God is the same yesterday, today, and tomorrow. He is the same as He was with Abraham, Joseph, and Moses. He is no different from the God whom Peter and Paul knew and followed. His glory, majesty, and divine character have remained constant since eternity past. And He will continue to be our unchanging Anchor of perfection for all eternity. We can count on God, completely and absolutely! Trust Him today with your whole heart.

# Readers' Guide

## For Personal Reflection or Group Discussion

Q uestions are an inevitable part of life. Proud parents ask their new baby, "Can you smile?" Later they ask, "Can you say 'Mama'?" "Can you walk to Daddy?" The early school years bring the inevitable, "What did you learn at school today?" Later school years introduce tougher questions, "If X equals 12 and Y equals –14, then …?" Adulthood adds a whole new set of questions. "Should I remain single or marry?" "How did things go at the office?" "Did you get a raise?" "Should we let Susie start dating?" "Which college is right for Kyle?" "How can we possibly afford to send our kids to college?"

This book raises questions, too. The following study guide is designed to (1) maximize the subject material and (2) apply biblical truth to daily life. You won't be asked to solve any algebraic problems or recall dates associated with obscure events in history, so relax. Questions asking for objective information are based solely on the text. Most questions, however, prompt you to search inside your soul, examine the circumstances that surround your life, and decide how you can best use the truths communicated in the book.

Honest answers to real issues can strengthen your faith, draw you closer to the Lord, and lead you into fuller, richer, more joyful, and productive daily adventures. So confront each question head-on and expect the One who is the answer for all of life's questions and needs to accomplish great things in your life.

## CHAPTER 1: CAN WE REALLY KNOW GOD?

1. What is meant by "God's character"? What all does this encompass?

2. What are some of the ways we can get to know God better? Name one or two ways that are especially meaningful to you.

3. Karl Marx did not believe in God; Martin Luther was convinced of God's existence. Can you think of two well-known modern-day figures whose faith in God, or lack thereof, affects their decisions and actions?

4. In what ways are our perceptions of God—either accurate or inaccurate—shaped and influenced?

## CHAPTER 2: KNOWING GOD CAN CHANGE YOUR LIFE

1. John Newton, a former slave trader, was radically changed when he became a Christian. Do you know someone who experienced dramatic change when he or she came to faith in Jesus?

2. What misconceptions about God have you had in the past, and how were they corrected?

3. Developing intimacy with God is a growth process. What has helped you most in this process?

4. Some people find it difficult to develop an intimate relationship with God because He is a Spirit—He does not have a body we can see and touch. Is this an issue for you? Why or why not?

## CHAPTER 3: HOW TO KNOW GOD

1. It is not possible to really know God without listening to Him. What prevents you from hearing God's voice? How can you better listen to Him?

2. According to Dr. Bright, "One way that we demonstrate our sincerity in seeking God is by our commitment to reading His Word." How would you rate your commitment to reading the Bible? What would help you to be even more consistent?

3. What did Jesus mean when He said, "Whoever has my commands and obeys them, he is the one who loves me" (John 14:21 NIV). Why are love and obedience so closely linked?

4. How do you think about your own life when viewed in light of eternity? Do you find it discouraging or motivating to know that our lives are brief interludes in the vast scope of eternity?

5. "Though [God] does not *need* us," Dr. Bright says, "He wants us to be involved with Him." In what ways are you involved in God's plan for mankind? In what ways would you *like* to be involved in the future?

## CHAPTER 4: GOD IS THREE PERSONS IN ONE

1. Is the concept of the Trinity—God in three forms—difficult for you to understand? Is there something that has helped you grasp this challenging concept?

2. As the author says, "This truth [the Trinity] is one of the most important aspects of God's relationship with us." Why is this so?

3. How has the Holy Spirit been present and active in your life? What evidence have you seen of the Spirit's help?

## CHAPTER 5: TRUSTING GOD COMPLETELY

1. The author states, "Sometimes we do not trust God because of negative life experiences that caused us to be untrusting of *anybody*." Is this true for you? Is it difficult for you to trust God because of past experiences?

2. The only way to overcome a lack of trust is to deeply understand who God is. How exactly can a true understanding of God help us develop trust in Him?

3. How would you rate your ability to trust God completely? What would allow you to trust Him even more?

4. How do you react to the statement "Because God is love, He is unconditionally committed to your well-being"?

5. "[God] is totally committed to His relationship with you," Dr. Bright writes, "so you can experience the many blessings of His grace and goodness." What blessings have you experienced in the past year?

## CHAPTER 6: GOD IS ALL-POWERFUL

1. Many people are skeptical about God's willingness to become intimately involved in their affairs. Do you sense that God is intimately involved in *your* life? How so?

2. Isaiah wrote, "All the nations of the world are nothing in comparison with him" (40:15). How does this declaration compare with the prevailing belief in our country today?

3. The author says, "No matter what happens anywhere in the world at any moment, God is always in control." How do you respond to that statement in light of the many disasters and wars throughout the world?

## Chapter 7: God Is Ever-Present

1. In this chapter, the author likens the Holy Spirit to wind. In what ways is the Spirit like wind? In what ways is He not?

2. Sometimes we feel God is not present with us in the midst of problems, but emotions can be misleading. Can you think of a time when you felt God was not with you? How can you gain the assurance that the Lord is, in fact, with you always?

3. Isaiah 43:1 states, "The Lord who created you says: 'Do not be afraid, for I have ransomed you. I have called you by name; you are mine.'" How do you respond to the fact that God called you by name?

4. As our Creator, God custom-designed us for a unique purpose. Do you have a clear sense of purpose and calling in life? If not, what would help you achieve that?

5. Verses such as the following unnerve some people: "The Lord is watching everywhere, keeping his eye on both the evil and the good" (Proverbs 15:3). What about you? How do you respond to the fact that God knows *everything*?

## CHAPTER 8: GOD IS SOVEREIGN

1. Our society champions qualities such as independence, autonomy, and self-sufficiency. How do these traits stack up against biblical admonitions and commandments?

2. Recall some of the earthly kings you have studied about or seen depicted in films. How are they like and unlike God, the King of kings? What are some of the key attributes of our King, the Lord of heaven and earth?

3. Dr. Bright states, "Part of our problem with accepting God's authority is that we have lost our concept of majesty." What do you think he means? How can we better understand God's majesty?

## CHAPTER 9: GOD IS HOLY

1. People in our society use many euphemisms to describe God, such as "the man upstairs" or "a supreme being." In what other ways do people diminish God's holiness and supremacy? How can you help to restore the reverence and respect due to our magnificent God?

2. The author says that "holy living involves a daily decision to surrender to the lordship of Christ." What exactly does *surrender* mean? How do you surrender to the lordship of Christ?

3. Solomon said, "Fear of the LORD is the beginning of wisdom. Knowledge of the Holy One results in understanding" (Proverbs 9:10). What is the relationship between fear of the Lord and wisdom? Can you have one without the other?

## CHAPTER 10: GOD IS ABSOLUTE TRUTH

1. What is meant by the term *absolute truth*? How can we know if something is absolutely true?

2. In our modern era, many people believe that truth is relative—it can change according to circumstances and differing perspectives. Can you identify some examples of this within our society?

3. Jesus promised, "If you hold to my teaching, you are really my disciples. Then you will know the truth, and the truth will set you free" (John 8:31–32 NIV). What is the relationship between truth and freedom? How does truth set us free?

## CHAPTER 11: GOD IS RIGHTEOUS

1. Can you think of a moral issue that was viewed as clearly wrong a few decades ago but is acceptable today? Why do certain standards of morality change over time?

2. King David wrote, "The LORD is righteous in all his ways and loving toward all he has made" (Psalm 145:17 NIV). How do those two aspects of God's character—righteousness and love—complement each other? What might happen if God had one of those qualities without the other?

3. "Our righteousness does not depend on what we do," Dr. Bright asserts, "but on whom we place our faith." What do you think he means by that? What is the role of personal responsibility in pursuing righteousness?

## CHAPTER 12: GOD IS JUST

1. The concept of justice has become blurred in our increasingly immoral society. How would you define justice? Think of an example of either *justice* or *injustice* that occurred recently.

2. Perhaps you know someone whose lifestyle does not reflect God's values, and yet the person is seemingly happy and successful. This is nothing new, since the Old Testament prophet Jeremiah once asked God, "Why are the wicked so prosperous? Why are evil people so happy?" (12:1). How would you respond? Why, as Jeremiah asked, does God allow wicked people to prosper?

3. Most people would prefer to focus on God's love and compassion while forgetting about His anger and wrath. Why is it important to remember God's wrath? How might God's "righteous anger" influence our own thoughts and behaviors?

## CHAPTER 13: GOD IS LOVE AND MERCY

1. Jesus declared, "'Love the Lord your God with all your heart and with all your soul and with all your mind.' This is the first and greatest commandment" (Matthew 22:37–38 NIV). How do you think those three aspects of loving God—with your heart, soul, and mind—are different and distinct from each other?

2. This chapter tells the story of when Jesus reached out to Zacchaeus, the greedy and despised tax collector. Who are the outcasts, the despised people, of our society? How might Christians better reach out to them?

3. The theme woven throughout this chapter is this: Because God is love, He is unconditionally committed to your well-being. In what ways is God currently working to improve and enrich your life?

4. Dr. Bright says that God's "mercy also means that He will discipline us as a father disciplines his child." Since God is not physically present with us, how does He discipline us?

5. The Gospels are filled with examples of how Jesus was moved with compassion to help those who were sick, suffering, and needy. Is there someone you know who demonstrates this kind of Christlike compassion and mercy? In what ways is this person inspirational to you?

## CHAPTER 14: GOD IS FAITHFUL

1. Although most Christians know that God has promised us all the strength and help we will ever need, many try to "go it alone" during times of trouble. Why is this? Why do many people fail to seek God's help?

2. The writer of Hebrews declared, "Without wavering, let us hold tightly to the hope we say we have, for God can be trusted to keep his promise" (10:23). What is the *hope* that your faith provides you? What is the link between God's faithfulness and our hope?

3. Is there a situation in your life in which you need God's help and protection? What would allow you to gain further assurance of His faithfulness to you?

4. Are you someone who enjoys change or resists it? How might this affect your attitude toward our never-changing, always-consistent God?

5. The psalmist said, "The LORD's plans stand firm forever; his intentions can never be shaken" (33:11). What are some of God's intentions for mankind? What are some of His intentions for your life?

## CHAPTER 15: LIVE IT!

1. Dr. Bright tells of flying in an airplane and placing his trust in the pilot, a total stranger. In what other ways do we trust people even though we know little or nothing about them?

2. What experiences have you had that prove God's faithfulness and dependability? What assurance do past experiences provide as you look to the future?

3. According to the author, "There is nothing more important to victorious living than what we believe to be true about God." What exactly do you think he means? How does this statement relate to your own life?

# Appendix A

# Because of Who God Is, You Can Face Any Situation

1. Because *God is a personal Spirit,* you can seek intimate fellowship with Him.

2. Because *God is all-powerful,* He can help you with anything.

3. Because *God is ever-present,* He is always with you.

4. Because *God knows everything,* you can go to Him with all your questions and concerns.

5. Because *God is sovereign,* you can joyfully submit to His will.

6. Because *God is holy,* you can devote yourself to Him in purity, worship, and service.

7. Because *God is absolute truth,* you can believe what He says and live accordingly.

8. Because *God is righteous,* you can live by His standards.

9. Because *God is just,* you can be sure He will always treat you fairly.

10. Because *God is love,* He is unconditionally committed to your well-being.

11. Because *God is merciful,* He forgives you of your sins when you sincerely confess them.

12. Because *God is faithful,* you can trust Him to always keep His promises.

13. Because *God never changes,* your future is secure and eternal.

# Appendix B

## God's Word on Trusting Him

Following are selected Scripture references that were presented throughout the text of this book. We encourage you to sit down with your Bible and review these verses in their context, prayerfully reflecting upon what God's Word tells you about the importance and joy of trusting Him.

**CHAPTER 1**

Romans 1:17

**CHAPTER 3**

John 4:24

John 3:3–6

1 Corinthians 2:10

Jeremiah 29:13

Hebrews 11:6

Psalm 119:15–16

John 14:21

**Chapter 4**

Genesis 1:26

**CHAPTER 6**

Isaiah 40:26

Isaiah 40:15

Daniel 4:35

Romans 16:20

Isaiah 46:10

Job 42:2

Isaiah 14:26

1 Corinthians 1:24

Ephesians 1:19–20

Philippians 4:13

Ephesians 3:20

**CHAPTER 7**

Acts 17:28

Hebrews 4:13

1 Corinthians 3:16

Psalm 139:8–10

Isaiah 43:1–3

Romans 8:38–39

Isaiah 46:9–10

Psalm 139:1–6
Proverbs 15:3
Jeremiah 29:11
Romans 11:33–34
1 Corinthians 10:13
James 1:5–7

**CHAPTER 8**

Psalm 24:8–10
1 Chronicles
  29:11–12
Daniel 2:21
Proverbs 19:21
Romans 8:28

**CHAPTER 9**

Romans 8:1–4
Exodus 15:11
Psalm 96:9
Psalm 2:11
Proverbs 9:10
Psalm 5:4
1 John 2:1–2
1 Peter 1:15
Galatians 2:20
Exodus 20:3–5
1 John 5:21

**CHAPTER 10**

2 Timothy 3:16
Numbers 23:19

Exodus 34:1
John 17:17
John 14:6
John 18:37
John 14:16–17
John 8:31–32

**CHAPTER 11**

Psalm 145:17
Psalm 119:137
Psalm 116:5
Romans 3:22–25
Ephesians 4:22–24

**CHAPTER 12**

Jeremiah 17:10
Deuteronomy 32:4
Psalm 7:11
Psalm 90:8–11
Ecclesiastes 12:14
Galatians 6:7
Deuteronomy
  32:35
Romans 2:5–8
Revelation
  20:11–15
2 Corinthians 5:10
Colossians 3:23–24

**CHAPTER 13**

1 John 4:8

Psalm 100:5
Luke 19:5
Ephesians 1:4–5
1 John 3:1
1 John 4:10
Matthew 22:37–38
Romans 3:23
James 5:11
Romans 6:23
1 Peter 2:24
Isaiah 49:13
John 8:11
Matthew 5:7
Matthew 6:15

**CHAPTER 14**

Psalm 89:8
1 Thessalonians
  5:24
Hebrews 10:23
2 Corinthians 1:20
2 Thessalonians
  3:3
1 John 1:9
1 Corinthians
  1:7–9
James 1:17
Isaiah 40:6–8
Psalm 33:11

# About the Author

DR. BILL BRIGHT, fueled by his passion to share the love and claims of Jesus Christ with "every living person on earth," was the founder and president of Campus Crusade for Christ. The world's largest Christian ministry, Campus Crusade serves people in 191 countries through a staff of 26,000 full-time employees and more than 225,000 trained volunteers working in some sixty targeted ministries and projects that range from military ministry to inner-city ministry.

Bill Bright was so motivated by what is known as the Great Commission, Christ's command to carry the gospel throughout the world, that in 1956 he wrote a booklet titled *The Four Spiritual Laws*, which has been printed in 200 languages and distributed to more than 2.5 billion people. Other books Bright authored include *Discover the Book God Wrote, God: Discover His Character, Come Help Change Our World, The Holy Spirit: The Key to Supernatural Living, Life Without Equal, Witnessing Without Fear, Coming Revival, Journey Home,* and *Red Sky in the Morning.*

In 1979 Bright commissioned the *JESUS* film, a feature-length dramatization of the life of Christ. To date, the film has been viewed by more than 5.7 billion people in 191 countries and has become the most widely viewed and translated film in history.

Dr. Bright died in July 2003 before the final editing of this book. But he prayed that it would leave a legacy of his love for Jesus and the power of the Holy Spirit to change lives. He is survived by his wife, Vonette; their sons and daughters-in-law; and four grandchildren.

# THE LIFETIME TEACHINGS OF

Written by one of Christianity's most respected and beloved teachers, this series is a must for every believer's library. Each of the books in the series focuses on a vital aspect of a meaningful life of faith: trusting God, accepting Christ, living a spirit-filled life, intimacy with God, forgiveness, prayer, obedience, supernatural thinking, giving, and sharing Christ with others.

Dr. Bill Bright was the founder of Campus Crusade for Christ Intl., the world's largest Christian ministry. He commissioned the JESUS film, a documentary on the life of Christ that has been translated into more than 800 languages.

## EACH BOOK INCLUDES A CELEBRITY-READ ABRIDGED AUDIO CD!

 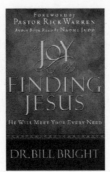 

Joy of Trusting God
Foreword by Billy Graham
Audio by John Tesh
0-78144-246-X

Joy of Finding Jesus
Foreword by Pastor
Rick Warren
Audio by Naomi Judd
0-78144-247-8

Joy of Spirit-Filled Living
Foreword by Kay Arthur
Audio by Ricky Skaggs
0-78144-248-6

# Dr. Bill Bright

FOUNDER OF CAMPUS CRUSADE FOR CHRIST

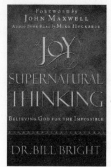

Joy of Supernatural Thinking
Foreword by John Maxwell
Audio by Gov. Mike Huckabee
0-78144-253-2

Joy of Dynamic Giving
Foreword by Charles Stanley
Audio by John Schneider
0-78144-254-0

Joy of Sharing Jesus
Foreword by Pat Robertson
Audio by Kathie Lee Gifford
0-78144-255-9

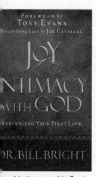

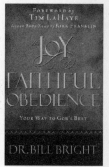

Joy of Intimacy with God
Foreword by Tony Evans
Audio by Amy Grant
0-78144-249-4

Joy of Total Forgiveness
Foreword by Gary Smalley
Audio by Janine Turner
0-78144-250-8

Joy of Active Prayer
Foreword by Max Lucado
Audio by Joni Earekcson Tada
0-78144-251-6

Joy of Faithful Obedience
Foreword by Tim LaHaye
Audio by Kirk Franklin
0-78144-252-4

## Collect all 10 of These Foundational Works!

# The Word at Work Around the World

A vital part of Cook Communications Ministries is our international outreach Cook Communications Ministries International (CCMI). Your purchase of this book, and of other books and Christian-growth products from Cook, enables CCMI to provide Bibles and Christian literature to people in more than 150 languages in 65 countries.

Cook Communications Ministries is a not-for-profit, self-supporting organization. Revenues from sales of our books, Bible curricula, and other church and home products not only fund our U.S. ministry, but also fund our CCMI ministry around the world. One hundred percent of donations to CCMI go to our international literature programs.

CCMI reaches out internationally in three ways:

• Our premier International Christian Publishing Institute (ICPI) trains leaders from nationally led publishing houses around the world.

• We provide literature for pastors, evangelists, and Christian workers in their national language.

• We reach people at risk—refugees, AIDS victims, street children, and famine victims—with God's Word.

## Word Power, God's Power

Faith Kidz, RiverOak, Honor, Life Journey, Victor, NexGen — every time you purchase a book produced by Cook Communications Ministries, you not only meet a vital personal need in your life or in the life of someone you love, but you're also a part of ministering to José in Colombia, Humberto in Chile, Gousa in India, or Lidiane in Brazil. You help make it possible for a pastor in China, a child in Peru, or a mother in West Africa to enjoy a life-changing book. And because you helped, children and adults around the world are learning God's Word and walking in his ways.

Thank you for your partnership in helping to disciple the world. May God bless you with the power of his Word in your life.

*For more information about our international ministries, visit www.ccmi.org.*